THE ATLANTIC CRITICAL STUDIES

William Congreve's *The Way of the World*

RATRI RAY

ATLANTIC
PUBLISHERS & DISTRIBUTORS (P) LTD

Published by
ATLANTIC
PUBLISHERS & DISTRIBUTORS (P) LTD
7/22, Ansari Road, Darya Ganj, New Delhi-110002
Phones : +91-11-40775252, 40775214, 23273880, 23275880
Fax : +91-11-23285873
Web : www.atlanticbooks.com
E-mail : orders@atlanticbooks.com

Branch Office: Chennai
Phones : +91-44-48531784, 28291383
E-mail : chennai@atlanticbooks.com

Printed & bound in India by Atlantic Print Services

Preface

The study-aids available in England and America, among other places, form the basis of *The Atlantic Critical Studies* which is primarily meant to cater to the needs of the students of English literature in Indian universities. The students in India pursuing English literature in their Honours and Post-graduation courses have to study under various constraints like non-availability of relevant critical books, dearth of foreign and Indian journals, inaccessibility to good and well-equipped libraries, among others. Although, Internet is of great help to the students these days, yet the plethora of information it brings before them often confuses them and they end up choosing a lot of irrelevant material which shifts the focus away from the topic or theme under discussion.

The books under *The Atlantic Critical Studies* fill the gap between the requirements and availability, and help the students by providing them quality material pertinent to their academic pursuits. The series covers authors and their works that are widely prescribed in Indian universities. This was necessary considering a regular demand for books that critically examine these authors and their works. The books in the series discuss all the major aspects of the works, besides providing sufficient information on the authors and the period in which they wrote. This makes each book in the series self-sufficient and of great benefit to the students. The scholarly authors who have prepared the books in the series have used authentic sources and taken special care to combine lucidity and profundity in their treatment of the texts.

The References in each chapter and the Select Bibliography at the end of the book are meant to help the students in making further study in specific areas if they want to.

The books in *The Atlantic Critical Studies* will also help researchers besides students and teachers of English literature.

Ratri Ray

Introduction

Congreve's time is known as the Restoration Era which is rich in literary output. The period produced figures like Milton on one hand and on the other satirists like Dryden and Pope (a bit later). Besides these titanic figures, it also produced a host of dramatists who wrote plays very different from the Elizabethan and Jacobean plays—tragedies and comedies in poetry. Congreve belonged to this group. He is an entirely Restoration figure as he was born ten years after the Restoration itself. This term itself means the Restoration of King Charles II to the throne of England. He had led the life of a gentleman, not that of a nobleman and had produced, besides a number of other works, four comedies of manners and his fame rests on these. This literary fame is of a high order, for he is, without question, the best of the dramatists. His contemporaries had put him on a very high pedestal though posterity has not. Dryden went so far as to compare him with Shakespeare:

> Heaven, that but once was prodigal before
> To Shakespeare gave as much, she could not give him more.[1]

Out of the four plays that brought him fame overnight, the one which is to be studied, *The Way of the World* is the best. Dr. Johnson has bestowed high praise on him, saying that he was an entirely original writer, and did not borrow his plots from others.

Bonamy Dobrée, in his Introduction to *Restoration Comedy,* has divided comedy into three varieties: Critical Comedy, "Free" comedy, and Great Comedy. Of these, the first is the largest group. Dobrée talks about comedy right from classical times onwards. After giving a brief introduction to the nature of the type of comedy he sums up its aims:

> Its object is to damp enthusiasm, to prick illusions. It is in a sense prig-drama, it flatters the vanity of the spectator, for whose amusement the weaknesses of his friends are held up.[2]

As we shall see, the attitude in *The Way of the World* is very much the same. It has to be pointed out that these three categories given by Dobrée are not mutually exclusive. The characteristics of one might, even should, overlap with the others and most of the plays show the characteristics of more than one.

The second of Dobrée's categories contain those plays that do not have the element of satire or morality in them. They are free of criticism and provide us with entertainment and laughter. Laughter, indeed, is the main ingredient of such plays. Dobrée says that no valuation is there in such comedies and he cites the plays of Etherege among the moderns and Aristophanes among the ancients: Congreve's plays have the element of laughter in them but moral valuation is definitely there. Only a few dialogues here and there can be said to have just entertainment value, but not entire plays as such.

The third category is the most serious one and comprises the great comedies in literature. The comedies of this category are so serious as to hover at the brink of tragedy. Plays like Ben Jonson's *Volpone* and the problem plays of Shakespeare like *Measure for Measure* and *Troilus and Cressida* are like this. Congreve's plays, however perfect, do not reach up to this standard.

Congreve's plays, therefore, belong to the first of Dobrée's categories, that of critical comedies—plays containing moral evaluation of life and society. Dobrée calls such plays "a social corrective" and that is what *The Way of the World* is.

References

1. Quoted by Dobrée, B., Restoration Comedy: 1660-1720, O.U.P. 1970 rpt. p. 121.
2. *Ibid*., p. 11.

Contents

1

The Background

Congreve's time, the Restoration Age, is different indeed from the preceding Cromwellian Age or the following Age of Reason. He came when the changes ushered in by the Restoration had already become a part of life, but the Age of Reason had not yet properly begun. He is a transitional figure. The period saw the restoration not only of monarchy, but of the feudal spirit as well. The landed gentry, woefully neglected in Cromwell's time, came back to power. This was to his advantage since he wanted to be looked upon as a "gentleman" just as he wanted literary fame.

(A) THE SOCIO-POLITICAL BACKGROUND

The Restoration of Charles II to the throne of England is the most important political event of the time. He had fled to France when Charles I was beheaded. In 1660, he came back to England and everything underwent a radical change. The lords and nobles who had been out of favour were in high favour now, and the landed gentry was back in power whether in the Court or in the country, they became the acknowledged leader of life. Their hereditary position of authority was restored to them.

There were two political parties: the Whig and the Tory. The Tory were the loyal followers of the King and they supported the ancient customs of the country and that of the Anglican Church. The Whigs were mostly the descendants of the Roundheads, i.e. Cromwell's men and they were in touch with the commercial class. This was the importance in the long run because of new scientific inventions taking place which were encouraged by the world of commerce. These inventions were encouraged by this world. As G.M. Trevelyan says:

> The uses to which science might be turned in agriculture, industry, navigation, medicine and engineering, appealed to the practical English mind.[1]

The Royal Society was founded under the patronage of the King. It prospered because his cousin Prince Rupert was interested in scientific pursuits. This interest itself made an interesting compromise with religion which was of benefit to both. The Bishop of London himself wrote a manifesto about its aims and characteristics. It says that scientific enquiry was to be made in all subjects except two:

> These two subjects, God and the Soul, being only forborne.[2]

This easily put the scientists above religious controversy, and they could carry on their researches.

The way in which the court encouraged the theatre can be praised, but not whole heartedly, because there was an anomaly here. The court patronized the theatre, but the King and the nobles had been influenced by the French Court which was profligate and extravagant. They had also been in exile for decades, their education had been neglected and family life almost destroyed, they lacked the stability of a wholesome home life. They had been also demoralized by all the humiliations and privations they had suffered, so nothing was sacred to them. This was not true for all of England but in the court, it was so and the court led the country. The nobility of the court had no belief in anything as they had seen hypocrisy everywhere:

> What makes all doctrines plain and clear?
> About two hundred pounds a year.
> And that which was proved true before
> Prove false again? two hundred more.[3]

It was Samuel Butler who wrote this, a contemporary of Congreve. A disbelief in virtue was the hallmark of the courtier. As this was the crowd patronising the stage, the drams reflected this attitude. However, this period of indifference to morality did not last. By the time Congreve came to write the worst was over. This point will be treated again in the section on Restoration drama.

Trade was also encouraged by the court. The national policy encouraged the increase of production for markets at home and abroad. This occurred at every level, from agriculture to industry, corn production and the manufacture of cloth. The Parliament passed strict laws about export and import in order to facilitate farmer, big and small, as well as manufacturers. It was in coal mining however that change was the most apparent. Mining had yet to attain the proportions of early nineteenth century which is known as the "age of coal and iron", but it had become widespread. It had a definite part to play in the increase of national wealth and the life of a large section of society—those who lived above ground as well as those who got their livelihood from under it. It is true that those who worked in the mines led a miserable life. This created a new class of people who were segregated from others. But artisans and farmers led a good communal life, even if they were poor, with their neighbours. Miners were, however, separated from others by virtue of their profession. They became a different class.

Coming to the city of London, its growth during the Restoration period is truly amazing. By 1700, London by itself housed more than a tenth of the population of England itself. This was being continually augmented by the coming of immigrants and the consequent inflow of wealth from outside. London suffered two mishaps at this time, the "Plague of London" and the "Great Fire". The plague in 1665 was the last such and in 1666 this was followed by the Great Fire which raged for no less than five days. After all this however, the city was built up at an amazing rate. By the time Congreve was born both the events were in the past and had become horrible memories. With the growth of the city also came the curse that is there in all great cities—slums had started. London had lost a fifth of its population because of the plague and the Great Fire but this was quickly made up. Due to the fire, the medieval and Tudor aspect had been lost and a more modern city was built with St. Paul's Cathedral as its focal point. In all, eighty-one churches had been burnt and therefore a great cathedral was built. It is the greatest work of Sir Christopher Wren. It took no less than thirty-five years to build and to this day it remains the greatest glory of Queen Anne's reign.

Chronological Table

1660 – Monarchy is restored. Royal Society created.

'62 – The King marries Catherine of Braganza.

'65 – The world's first scientific journal. *Philosophical Transactions of the Royal Society* pub.

– Newton develops differential calculus.

– Five-day Great Fire.

'68 – William Penn imprisoned for questioning the doctrine of Trinity.

– King Charles leases City of Bombay to East India Co.

'70 – Treaty of Dover promising help to France against Spain and the Dutch Republic signed.

– Wren begins designing churches.

'73 – Parliament passes Test Act making it impossible for Catholics to hold offices in England.

'75 – Greenwich Royal Observatory founded.

'77 – Mary, niece of the King, marries William of Orange.

'79 – King dissolves Parliament. Rebellion of Scottish covenanter ruthlessly put down.

'81 – King calls his fifth parliament.

'82 – Newton explains Kepler's laws. Halley's Comet observed.

'85 – Charles II dies. Succeeded by James II.

'86 – Newton's *Principia Mathematica*.

'88 – James II issues second Declaration of Liberty of Conscience. He flees to France.

'89 – England offers the throne to William of Orange and his wife Mary. They accede to the throne.

'94 – Bank of England started.

'96 – Trials for Treason Act passed.

(B) THE LITERARY BACKGROUND

Congreve's time, the Restoration Age, is a transitional time, with the great personality of Milton hovering over it. The Restoration, a political event, yet influenced literature most heavily. As the Puritan government collapsed, it brought about an excess of light-heartedness and immorality that was encouraged by the court. But all this cynicism is seen in the comedies, but not in the other forms. Bonamy Dobrée sums it up:

> The most hasty student of history regards the quarter-century succeeding the Restoration as one of unbridled license.... But this, of course was not true of the whole community.[4]

Milton was the greatest figure. He lived and wrote his greatest and best work during this time, but he cannot be said to be a Restoration man. He retired directly after the Restoration and working quietly, produced *Paradise Lost* and *Paradise Regained* and *Samson Agonistes*. None of these give any impression of his time. Perhaps this is because he continued from an earlier era. An almost absolute break with the past occurred at this time. The subject of literature in addition to its style became so different in spirit that this age is often said to be the opposite of the Elizabethan. There was the influence of French literature too. It was the time of Molière and Racine and both of them were highly influential. As a result, two new types of play came into existence. Both French and classical models were copied in tragedy and thus the "heroic tragedy" came into existence, of which Dryden's *All for Love* is the best. In comedies of course there came the comedy of manners. All these influences caused priority to be given to 'polish and a good finish':

> Of all these arts in which the wise excel,
> Nature's chief masterpiece is writing well;
> No writing lifts exalted man so high
> As sacred and soul-breathing Poesy.
> No kind of work requires so nice a touch
> And, if well finished nothing shines so much.[5]

Satire came through the imitation of the classics. Dryden's political satires were typical of the time, but he wrote poems on the topic of religion too—an issue vexing everyone at that time. *Absalom and Achitophel* and *The Medal* are both political satires whereas *Religio Laici* and *The Hind and the Panther* are on religious topics. Dryden produced a lot and was a versatile genius who could successfully try any form. He could write convincingly opposite sides of the same topic. For example, *Religio Laici* supported the Anglican church while *The Hind and the Panther* supported Catholicism. As he was a versatile poet, he took up verse tragedy and produced *All for Love* imitating Shakespeare's *Antony and Cleopatra*. He has also written one of the most important essays on literary criticism, *Essay of Dramatic Poesie*.

Many other dramatists also wrote heroic tragedies, the best among them being Thomas Otway whose finest work is *Venice Preserv'd* . Another writer was Nathaniel Lee. *Nero*, *Sophonisba* and *Mithridates* are some of his works. He is known as a writer of "the raving style".

Besides Dryden, Samuel Butler is the only poet of any strength. His only work *Hudibras* is a verse satire. It is written in octosyllabic couplets and is highly topical. All the other long poems were in heroic couplets as developed by Edmund Waller. It was Dryden however who really established it, for all his poems are in this measure. Pope, in the succeeding age, brought it to perfection. Of the other verse forms, the most important is the blank verse, which underwent the greatest change possible from Elizabethan blank verse in the hands of Milton. As a whole, poetry became "copy of Nature", and it became allied to truth:

> Allied thus to the intellectual revolution, poetry observed the "real" world, its social intercourse, its ethic and its temper.[6]

The prose of this time became subject to a remarkable development. There had been the great Elizabethan masters who modelled themselves deliberately after the classical writers and wrote a highly developed, sophisticated, and a literary academic prose. Now, however, prose became to be cultivated as a common medium of communication. The ideal of the Royal Society was of lucidity and simplicity and it naturally influenced prose. Addison, Swift had not come as yet but their way was being prepared. Dryden's *Essay* is easily a landmark as also is Bunyan. One important prose work has to be mentioned here, not for its literary value but for the tremendous impact it had. This was Jeremy Collier's *A Short View of the Immorality, and Profaneness of the English Stage*. It was not good prose, colloquial and at times even ungrammatical but it caused the closure of the play houses.

Now it is time to have a look at Restoration drama. It is one of the things that the entire court of Charles II patronized—the theatre. In fact, one of the first acts of the King was to issue a patent in the name of Killigrew, authorising him to open two play houses, in 1660. The courtly group was a profligate dissolute and cynical group, having no faith in God or man, as has been pointed out. They thought money related all-honour, chastily, honesty. Button wrote in *Hudibras*:

> What makes all doctrines plane and clear?
> About two hundred pounds a year.
> And that which was proved true before
> Prove false again? two hundred more.[7]

It is for this licentious, irreverent and vicious group that the theatre catered and the country followed the lead, portraying society very like the court.

(I) THE NATURE OF RESTORATION DRAMA

Apart from the change in morals, certain important changes had taken place in the theatre. One of them was that female roles came to be performed by women. Nell Gwynne's name is remembered. One of the reasons of Congreve's popularity was the presence of the famous actress Mrs Bracegirdle in them.

The courtiers did not believe in virtue but, rather, laughed at it. This attitude was reflected in Wycherley's play, *The Country Wife* with its outrageous plot became very popular. So were his other plays.

The main features of this kind of play (the comedy of manners, as it came to be called) are easily summed up. The authoritative and pioneering scholar in this field is definitely

Bonamy Dobrée. He has pointed out three essential features: its impurity, its realism and its style. Later critics also, but with little variation, follow his lead. As it is, comedy is usually based upon real life which is not a very attractive subject. So realism is often accompanied with disgust or mild satire and in the present case both are present. After all, Cicero had described comedy as "imitation of life, image of truth, mirror of custom."

First of all, there is the question of its impurity or licentiousness which was strenuously objected to at that time itself by Jeremy Collier in his essay *A Short View,* etc. Later Lamb too objected to it in his famous essay. He takes a more lenient attitude than Collier and says that ordinary rules of morality should not be applied because it is an "unmoral" world. About the characters, he says in a famous sentence:

> They have got out of Christendom into the land of cuckoldry—the utopia of gallantry.[8]

Much more serious still is the objection that the plays are "trivial, gross and dull," that they do not give any indication of the thought of the time. This objection however is not very valid because this comedy is by its very nature a portrayal of manners, not of ideas, so superficiality is expected and commendable.

In defence of this comedy, it has been said by Bonamy Dobrée that these plays actually express a "deep curiosity" about "sex-relationships" and a "desire to try new ways of living." This, though vaguely, relates it to the spirit of the time, the scientific curiosity that led to the founding of the Royal Society.

Its licentiousness is self-evident, and so is its realism, though Lamb has presented a different point of view. But it will be advisable, at this stage to give some critical opinion a bit later than Dobrée. A very scholarly work has been done by D.L. Hirst in this field. He defines *Comedy of Manners* thus:

> The subject of Comedy of manners is the way people behave, the manners they employ in a social context; the chief concerns of the characters are sex and money (and thus the inter-related topics of marriage, adultery and divorce); the style is distinguished by the refinement of

raw emotional expression and action in subtlety of wit and dialogue.[9]

This is a very comprehensive definition, covering every aspect of the play and later the author applies it to the plays he deals with. We shall come across his opinion on Congreve as we deal with the different aspects of *The Way of the World*.

(II) A CHRONOLOGICAL TABLE

In this table, only a very limited period of time has been covered. It starts ten years before Congreve's birth, with the Restoration in 1660 and ends in 1770 when, after producing *W.W.* to lukewarm reception he retired from literary life.

1660	–	Dryden's poem *Astraea Redux*.
	–	Patent issued in the name of Killigrew, authorizing him to open two play houses.
	–	Evelyn begins his Diary.
'63	–	Samuel Butler *Hudibras*.
'65	–	Dryden's play *The Indian Emperor.*
'66	–	Bunyan's *Grace Abounding*.
'67	–	Milton *Paradise Lost*.
'68	–	Etherege *She Wou'd if She Cou'd*
	–	Dryden *Essay of Dramatic Poesie*.
'71	–	Milton *Paradise Regained, Samson Agonistes*
	–	Wycherley *Love in a Wood*
'73	–	Dryden *Marriage á la Mode*
'74	–	Shadwell *The Enchanted Island* based on Shakespeare's *The Tempest*.
'75	–	Wycherley *The Country Wife*
'76	–	Dryden *Aurangzebe*, Etherege *Man of Mode*
'77	–	Wycherley *The Plain Dealer*
	–	Nathaniel Lee *The Rival Queens*
'78	–	Dryden *All for Love*, Bunyan *Pilgrim's Progress*
'79	–	Dryden and Nathaniel Lee *Oedipus*

'81	–	Dryden's poem *Absalom and Achitophel* and play *Spanish Fryar*
'82	–	Otway *Venice Preserv'd*
'92	–	Congreve *Incognita*
'94	–	Congreve *The Double Dealer*, Dryden *Love Triumphant*
'95	–	Congreve *Love for Love*, Locke's *Essay*
'96	–	Congreve *The Mourning Bride*, Vanbrugh *The Relapse*
'98	–	Jeremy Collier *A Short View of the Immorality, and Profaneness of the English Stage*
'99	–	Farquhar *Love in a Bottle*, Dryden *Fables*
'1700	–	*Way of the World*, Farquhar *The Constant Couple.*

References

1. Trevelyan, G.M., *Illustrated English Social History*, Vol. 2, Penguin Books, 1960, p. 217.
2. Quoted in *ibid.*, p. 217.
3. Quoted in *ibid.*, p. 221.
4. Dobrée, B., *op. cit.*, p. 17.
5. Quoted in Ford, B. ed. *From Dryden to Johnson*, Vol. 4, Penguin Books, 1960, pp. 52-53.
6. Humphreys, A.R., *The Literary Scene*, in *ibid.*, p. 80.
7. Please see Socio-Political Background above.
8. Quoted in Dobrée *op. cit.*, p. 22.
9. Hirst, D.L., *Comedy of Manners,* Methuen & Co. Ltd., London, 1979, p. 1.

2
Life and Works

(A) CONGREVE: A SHORT BIOGRAPHY (1670–1729)

Congreve was born in 1670 (though Dr. Johnson gives the date as 1672), fully ten years after the Restoration, and was a typical product of his period. Born near Leeds, he had an Irish upbringing. Dr. Johnson says that he belonged to a family that was so ancient that it could trace its ancestry back to before the Norman Conquest. He was the son of an army officer which means the family, though respectable, was not noble. This has to be pointed out as it was his ambition to be taken as a gentleman of high society, a man-about-town. Macaulay had drawn attention to this:

> Two kinds of ambition early took possession of his mind and often pulled it in opposite directions.... He longed to be a good writer. He longed to be a man of fashion. The history of his life is the history of a conflict between these two impulses.[1]

But it is not surprising that a man who could trace his ancestry beyond the Norman Conquest should want to be given the status of a gentleman.

His education was in Ireland, at Kilkenny school and later at Trinity College, Dublin. It was here that his life-long friendship with Swift began.

He came to England in 1688 and entered Middle Temple at London at the age of sixteen, according to Dr. Johnson. This institute was meant for lawyers, but no record exists of a legal practice on his part. An unsuccessful novel, *Incognita*, was published by him in 1692. Then he turned to the state. He produced four comedies during the next seven years. All of them except the last were successful on the stage. He worked in an administrative capacity as he became the joint manager of the Haymarket Theatre, along with Vanbrugh. It is a pity that he gave up writing at the age of thirty.

He had been appointed in many government jobs. He had become, one after another, the Commissioner for the licensing of hackney coaches (1695-1707), Commissioner for wine licensing (1705-14) and Secretary for Jamaica from 1714 onwards.

As a person he was careful to avoid politics and was a well-known figure in the fashionable and literary society of London. Among his intimate friends he numbered Swift, Dryden, Steele and Pope. They had great regard for him as can be understood when it is known that Pope had dedicated his *Iliad* to him. He had fulfilled his ambition, i.e. become a fashionable gentleman. Voltaire, when a young man, visited him in 1726. He was disappointed to find a fashionable gentleman, not a dramatist. His career as a dramatist lay twenty years behind him and he infinitely shocked Voltaire by saying that he wanted to be known "upon no other foot than that of a gentleman who led a life of plainness and simplicity." In reply to this, Voltaire said, "that if he had been only a gentleman he should not have come to visit him".

The fact remains that he was valued by his friends. He was a warm-hearted person. Though his comedies portray fools, his satire against them is very mild. Even then, he had said that instead of laughing at them one should pity them. If his friends loved him, he returned that too and he had said that he wanted "to feel very sensibly and silently for those I love." It is well known that he was one of the three "most honest-hearted, real good men, of the poetic members of the Kit-Kat Club." These opinions and many others such about him as a man prove that he was a man of sterling qualities. He became blind towards the end of his life. He remained a bachelor to the very end, though he had lived in close intimacy with Mrs. Bracegirdle. He died in 1729 and his funeral and burial was held at the Abbey with great pomp and ceremony.

The Chief Events of His Life

1670 – Born at Bardsey, near Leeds.

’85 – Goes to Trinity College, Dublin.

’92 – Publishes *Incognita*, under the name Cleophil.

– Translates the 11th Satire of Juvenal for Dryden’s translation.

– Writes complimentary verses for Dryden’s Persius: *On Mrs. Arabella Hunt Singing.*

’93 – *The Old Bachelor.*

’84 – *The Double Dealer.*

– Obtains a post in the Pipe office.

’95 – *The Mourning Must of Alexis.*

– *Love for Love, Ode to the King.*

– Letters to Dennis *Concerning Humour in Comedy.*

– Becomes Commissioner for Licensing Hackney Coaches.

’97 – *The Mourning Bride, The Birth of the Muse.*

’98 – *Amendments of Mr. Collier’s False and Imperfect Citations.*

1700 – *The Way of the World.*

’01 – *The Judgement of Paris, Ode for St. Cecilia’s Day.*

’04 – *Squire Trelooby*, an adaptation from *Monsieur de Pourceaugnac*, in collaboration with Vanbrugh and Walsh.

’05 – *The Tears of Amaryllis.*

– Is given a place in the Customs.

’06 – *A Pindaric Ode to the Queen* with *A Discourse on the Pindaric Ode.*

’10 – Pub. of his works, with *Semele.*

’14 – Place in the Customs bettered. Receives in addition the secretaryship of the Island of Jamaica.

’20 – Pope dedicates his *Iliad* to him.

'22	–	Steele dedicates to him his edition of Addison's *The Drummer.*
'26	–	Is visited by Voltaire.
1729	–	Dies, *Epistle to Lord Cobham* posthumously pub. written 1728.

(B) CONGREVE'S WORKS

Congreve's works consist of mainly the four comedies written in the mode of Restoration comedies and very little else. In these, he excels, but it can be seen in the short life-sketch given above that he had started his literary life with a novel, *Incognita*, in 1692. It did not succeed, and then he turned to the stage. He had already written *The Old Bachelor* (1693) four years ago and on the stage, it was an immediate success. He himself had said that he had written it "to amuse himself in a slow recovery from a fit of illness". This was followed quickly by *The Double Dealer* (1693). This brought him great fame as a dramatist. After seeing this, Dryden was overwhelmed and wrote, in a verse epistle, the lines comparing him with Shakespeare quoted earlier.

He went from success to success because his next play, *Love for Love* (1695) was a roaring success. It was highly popular and was also of great importance. This can be seen because when Betterton left Drury Lane with a whole group of artists and opened a new theatre at Lincoln's Inn Fields they opened with this play. After this he wrote a tragedy, *The Mourning Bride* (1697). This was very successful on the stage for the time being but is of no importance now. After this he produced his last work *The Way of the World* (1700). He lived for twenty more years but without producing any work of any merit. The only work worth mentioning after this was a farce adapted from Moliére in collaboration with Vanbrugh, *Squire Trelooby* (1704).

This does not, of course, mean that he did not write anything else. He wrote some poems but these were of little merit. Dr. Johnson criticised them, with justice, quite stringently.

When he had achieved maturity, society had become more stabilized than it formerly was. The licentious Restoration Age was soon to be succeeded by the Age of Reason and Congreve is midway between the two. When he is contrasted with Wycherley then the difference between his attitude and that of the preceding age can be properly seen. Wycherley, it is clear, hated and despised the men he saw and portrayed. Not so with Congreve for he was very mild. In the Dedication of *The Way of the World,* he says that the fools he portrayed:

> ...are of fools so gross...they are rather objects of Charity rather than contempt; and instead of moving our mirth, they ought very often to excite our compassion.[2]

What attracts the attention of the reader first is his style. The brilliance of his wit dazzles the reader and often he does not pay attention to anything else. He portrays, as was but usual in these plays, a person who is essentially a fool but wants to be taken for a wit—a would-be wit. But Congreve is so brilliant that often his fools seem to be as clever as the true wits of other dramatists. Pope had asked, "Tell me if Congreve's fools are fools indeed?" But in spite of this verbal pyrotechnics there is serious thought also. Coleridge had seen this and held that the plays were not just a light-hearted exposure of contemporary manners. It was Congreve's plays that had elicited the profound remark "wickedness is no subject for comedy" and he went on to say that Congreve made the mistake of dealing with wickedness in plays. Congreve is no mere light-hearted entertainer and he makes it clear in the Prologue in which he says:

> Some plot we think he has, and some new Thought
> Some Humour too, no Farce; but that is a fault.

Dryden, Wycherley and others portray characters that are full of vice and are indecent, but they are not morally wicked as Congreve's bad characters are. He is, after all, a serious critic of society. Bonamy Dobrée thinks that the lightness of this kind of play did not suit his grave temperament, it did not allow him to say what he wanted to say. No wonder he retired when only thirty.

It is time now to briefly introduce his other works. He, as is apparent from the chronological table of the chief events of his life, wrote, besides the four comedies on which his reputation rests, many other works, chiefly poems, and had hoped a lot from them. But they were actually quite inferior works as Dr. Johnson had made stringently clear. Here we shall concern ourselves with the three other comedies, *The Old Bachelor* (1693), *The Double Dealer* (1694), and *Love for Love* (1695).

The Old Bachelor (1693)

The play was taken very seriously as is evident from the three poems by admirers that precede it. Congreve makes his attitude to the play as a whole quite clear in the Prologue he wrote to it:

> A Play makes war, and Prologue is the Drum:
> Arm'd with keen Satire and pointed wit.
> We threaten you who for Judges sit.[3]

Looking at the title page of the play, one sees that in this very first play itself, Congreve has missed out none of the whole contingency of the comedy of manners characters: the true-loves (Bellmour and Belinda) and true-wits (Bellmour and Vainlove) the would-be wits (Sir Joseph Wittol), the braggart (Captain Bluffe), the doting husband (Fondlewife), the deceitful wife (Letitia), and of course the old bachelor of the title, secretly in love with a woman but unwilling to admit it (Heartwell). All these characters are true to the type and the plot, as is expected in such plays, proceeds by twists and turns to the desired end. It must be admitted that the plot is a little too full of pretences and betrayals but this is made clear in the very first scene of the play when the dialogue between the two true-wits Bellmour and Vainlove clarify their relationship with each other. Each furthers the other's cause by exchanging mistresses and thus deceiving each other with full knowledge of each other. It is a rather disgusting picture they present of their mutual relationship—an ugly, immoral relationship. Vainlove is perhaps the oddest character of all as he lives up to his name for he cannot be constant in his love. His beloved Araminta has to pretend to despise him and betray him in order to really capture him. Letitia, Fondlewife's wife, writes to him telling him that her husband will not be at home in the evening so he must put on the habit of a friar and go to her house. Most perversely Vainlove gives this work to Bellmour as he does not want to win a mistress so easily. Intrigue piles on intrigue, disguise on disguise and deceit on deceit till the very end. Even then there is no clear-cut ending with the union of true-loves.

Commenting on the different aspects of the play Dobrée first of all finds that it is the realm of ideas, that we are in contact with a thinker. This is because Bellmour talks of Socrates which makes Dobrée think that he is a thoughtful man.

Again talking about Heartwell, Dobrée finds food for thought in him:

> It strikes at the deepest disharmony in man's nature, and touches that bedrock of discordant impulses in the face of which, if we cannot ignore, we must either laugh of perish.[4]

This is to take a very serious view indeed of what seems to be Heartwell's diffidence and unwillingness to admit that he is in love which is not so extraordinary. Many men may, in real life as well as in literature, find themselves in a like position.

Looking at the only pair of true-loves in the play, Dobrée is reminded at once of a much later and very like pair, that of Mirabell and Millamant. Indeed, the comparison is inevitable. Pointing out the resemblance, Dobrée observes, again in serious vein:

> Here we have sex antagonism in full blast, the realism touched with just the necessary lightness and delicacy.[5]

Contrasting the charming verbal fencing between Bellmour and Belinda with the Heartwell-Silvia affair, he points out its seriousness—it is forthright and there is no finesse about it.

Referring to the minor scenes (e.g. those of Fondlewife) Dobrée compares Congreve with Ben Jonson and Terence and others but he is not always so serious in his remarks. He points to the fools, Sir Joseph and Captain Bluffe and says that:

> Congreve's skill as a manipulator of pure frolic is immediately seen; he could handle farce as well as anybody...we are in the realm of Elizabethan Comedy.[6]

It is indeed true what he says. While Sir Joseph can be a character out of Ben Jonson, Captain Bluffe is the braggart to the life. One comes across him again and again in Elizabethan comedy which is a robust and vigorous enjoyment of life.

We have been looking exclusively at the opinion of Dobrée on this play. Other writers, following the pioneer and revering tradition, agree with him. D.L. Hirst has some comments to make. A valuable comment is the one on the dance with which the play ends:

> The first play...ends with a dance which as in Shakespearean comedy celebrates the forthcoming marriages.[7]

The action of the play, however, is typical of the comedy of manners:

> Bellmour's comment on this situation reveals (with an appropriately neat turn of phrasing) the coolness of a moral debauchee.[8]

To adapt his phrase a little "amoral debauchery" exactly fits the temper of the play.

A few quotations from the play itself will be appropriate now to reveal its style, wit and the air of "amoral debauchery". Thus, Bellmour, the true-wit talks to Vainlove, another true-wit:

> Come, Come, leave Business to Idlers, and Wisdom to Fools; they have need of them: Wit, be my Faculty and Pleasure, my Occupation...Business is not my Element—I rowl in a higher Orb, and Dwell—
>
> Vainlove: In Castles i'th' Air of thy own building.[9]

This dialogue precedes an intrigue of adultery in which the two friends help each other. They cheerfully exchange mistresses with no sense of immorality. Indeed, it is almost the land of Cuckoldry, the Utopia of gallantry as Lamb called it. This is borne out by the way the treatment of love comes to be taken by us. We know that Bellmour and Belinda are in love. But we know it theoretically; the deep sincerity of true love is missing. It is missed even more in the Araminta-Vainlove intrigue. Araminta loves him sincerely, but it is so much wrapped up in subterfuges and deceits that the sincerity of Araminta's love does not come through to us. For example, Bellmour and Belinda talk:

> **Bellmour:** I have laid out such a world of love in your service, that you think you can never be able to pay me all: So shun me for the same reason that you would shun a dun.

> **Belinda:** Ay, on my Conscience, and the impertinent and troublesome of Duns—a Dun for Money will be quiet, when he sees his Debtor has not wherewithal—But a Dun for Love is an eternal Torment that never rests.[10]

This is very like the light-hearted badinage we shall find in *The Way of the World* and it does give an impression of love, but it is the only occasion and is belied by what goes before and after so that the impression of depth is utterly lacking.

It is not to be wondered at that this first play of Congreve's was such a success on the stage. It has all the ingredients that are necessary for a successful comedy of manners. Then there is Congreve's inimitable style that gives constant hints of better things to come in the later plays.

There are two songs in the play, one in Act II, sc. ix and another in III, x. It is followed by a "Dance of Antics" thus providing the element of spectacle, one of Aristotle's requirements. A Dance is also given at the end, signifying the forthcoming marriages as commented upon earlier. Another characteristic of the play is that often the scenes end with a Senecan couplet. The first of them comes at the end of I, v, said by Sharper:

> For Love's Island: I, for the Golden Coast
> May each succeed in what he wishes most.[11]

This, like a Senecan couplet, sums up the mood.

The play ends with an Epilogue spoken by Letitia, Fondlewife's wife. It does not have any very notable observations to make but is a light-hearted ending to a light-hearted play as is to be expected.

The Double Dealer

Congreve's next play *The Double Dealer* was also a roaring success on the stage. It was held in such high esteem that Dryden himself wrote a poem in praise of it. After praising him and saying he combined the qualities of other dramatists, Dryden gives the famous lines:

> Heav'n, that once was Prodigal before,
> To Shakespeare gave as much she could not give him more.[12]

This play is rather odd in that the moral lesson to be conveyed through it was written out first and then the play was built around it. He said:

> I designed the moral first...and to that moral I invented the fable.[13]

This presages an impression of artificiality in the play yet surprisingly enough, there is none. He says he took deliberate pains with the play, making the plot a strong one as it is a single-plotted play. Dobrée, with his characteristic clear-sightedness, pinpoints the difficulty about analysing the play:

> ...the difficulty is to arrive at that very subtle and elusive thing, the "idea" of the play, the dominant mood that led to its creation. This may be conveyed by the action, the delineation of character, or by the atmosphere which is the resultant of these combined with the wording.[14]

That is to say, Dobrée includes in this comprehensive sentence the plot, the characterization, and the style all of which help to assert, to communicate the main idea of the play. In this context, he makes a very penetrating remark. He says that Congreve tries to mingle two different strains: on one hand, there is the amoral world that Lamb talks of and on the other, the ordinary, realistic and domestic world. He gives several quotations from the play, one of which is particularly illuminating:

> For wisdom and honesty, give one cunning and hypocrisie;
> Oh, 'tis such a play, to angle for fair-faced fools.[15]

After remarking that such a character "is villainy itself" Dobrée contrasts it with the light-hearted world of the fops and fools, saying that it is "the very culmination of social tomfoolery." Both exist in this play and this contrast between the two worlds is something Congreve deliberately highlights.

Many are the intrigues that take place in this play—too many, as a matter of fact, for a single-plotted play. Maskwell is unmasked and thwarted, much in the tradition of humour plays. Touchwood is possessed by unreasoning rage to such an extent that he throws his wife out of the house and Lady Touchwood is in despair, so much so that one cannot help sympathising with her.

In other words, one is emotionally moved, not just intellectually stirred, and then Dobrée points out, Brisk says "This is all very surprising, let me perish" and with this remark, Congreve brings us back to the world where nothing is important—everything is taken lightly.

Dobrée finds Congreve to be in a serious mood in this play. Most of the time he is not in the mood of a comedy writer. This the case particularly with Mellefont-Maskwell intrigue. He treats both Maskwell and Lady Touchwood seriously—not with the good-humour of a comedy writer, nor with the detachment of a satirist. He treats them like a judge, punishing them for their faults. Characters like Touchwood, Mellefont and Cynthia are honest and likeable people, they represent the ordinary world, "models of the golden mean".

As a result of this severe attitude, his wit is not of a high standard. It is not, most of the time, like that of the true-wits but more like that of the wit-wouds. Yet in the very next sentence, paradoxically, Dobrée says:

> The dialogue is nearly always magnificent neat and blade-like, the delineation of the fops highly entertaining. Lady Plyant is perfect.[16]

When a critic like Dobrée is in two minds and flatly contradicts himself then it is no wonder that the common reader should be puzzled.

D.L. Hirst has a most interesting observation to make. According to him, most of the roles of *The Double Dealer* and *The Way of the World* were inspired by living persons:

> Maskwell is an ancestor of Fainall, the parts were both played by Betterton just as the heroines Araminta, Cynthia, Angelica and Millamant were created by Mrs. Bracegirdle whereas the roles of the more cunning and licentious women, Letitia, Lady Touchwood, Mrs. Frail and Mrs. Marwood were written for Mrs. Barry.[17]

This is a very revealing point—revealing about stage history as well as the art of characterization of Congreve. Moreover, he has almost the same observation to make about the plot. Maskwell is defeated by his own dupe. He is clever and has insight into human nature. His cynical observation about Lady Touchwood that love's thirst is easily quenched (very much like Vainlove's in *The Old Bachelor*). His defeat is doubly a defeat as it is in the hands of his dupe.

A few representative quotations from the text will make the atmosphere of the play clear. Mellefont and his friend Careless are the true-wits of the play and Maskwell is called a villain right in the beginning. He is "pretended friend to Mellefont, Gallant to Lady Touchwood and in love with Cynthia." When Mellefont and Careless talk with each other, it is as true-wits talk:

> *Careless*: Where are the women? I'm weary of guzling and begin to think them the better company.
>
> *Mellefont*: Then thy reason staggers, and thou'rt almost Drunk,
>
> C.: No Faith, but your Fools grow noisie—and if a Man must endure the Noise of Words without Sense, I think the women have more Musical Voices and become Nonsense better.[18]

This witty talk right in the beginning of the play is sustained throughout and already the impression that Congreve's fools talk almost as well as his true-wits is borne out by Brisk:

> Pshaw man when I say you spoil Company by leaving it,
> I mean you leave no body for the Company to laugh at.[19]

Mellefont acknowledges the wit of this remark by telling Brisk that his remark is a home-thrust. Things become even more hectic when two would-be wits talk each vying with the other for attention, trying to be wittier than each other:

> Lord Froth: Now when I laugh, I always Laugh alone.
>
> Brisk: I suppose that's because you laugh at your own jests, I'gad, ha, ha, ha.
>
> Ld. F.: He, he, he, I swear though, your Railing provokes me to a smile.
>
> Br.: Ay, my Lord, it's a sign I hit you in the Teeth, if you show them.
>
> Ld. F.: He, he, he, I swear that is so very pretty, I cannot forbear.[20]

In cases like these one may well ask, as Pope did "Tell me if Congreve's fools are fools indeed"? It becomes even more hilarious when a true-wit gets into the group, as Careless does here.

A few more things have to be pointed out. There is a song in the play, in II, iii—a conventional love-song and it ends the scene. There are also, as in *The Old Bachelor*, many Senecan couplets in the play. As usual, they serve often to end a scene. The first Act ends with Maskwell voicing his policy of deception:

> One Minute gives Invention to destroy
> What to rebuild, will a whole Age employ.[21]

The play is, from whatever point of view, a more polished work than *The Old Bachelor*, but less polished than *The Way of the World* but a worthy precursor of it. Its sparkling wit, its character-delineation, its plot, everything has given it a status of its own among comedies of this kind, of this age or later.

Love for Love

This, Congreve's third play, was highly popular in his day and was thought to be his best. It is a romantic play and its name proclaims its theme. It has less of the elements of comedies of manners than those of a romantic play, being more tolerant of human follies and more good-humoured. There can be no doubt about his attitude as he makes clear from the very beginning, in the Prologue itself:

> There's Humour, which for chearful friends we got,
> And for the thinking Party there's a Plot.
> ....
> Tho' Satire scarce dares grin, 'tis grown so mild
> Or only shows its Teeth, as if it smil'd.[22]

No better proof can be there of the good humour with which the play has been conceived and the lack of bitterness or savagery. Specially referring to Wycherley, he says again in the Prologue:

> Since the Plain—Dealer's Scene of Manly Rage
> Not one has dar'd to lash this crying Age
> This time, the Poet owns the Bold Essay
> Yet hopes there's no Ill-manners in his Play

> And he declares by me, he has designed
> Affront to none, but frankly speaks his Mind[23]

Here again it is quite clear that satire is not his aim.

As for the romantic nature of the play, again and again we find in it professions of deep and sincere love. Angelica says to Scandal:

> I fear my happiness depends upon the recovery of Valentine therefore I conjure you, as you are his Friend, and as you have compassion upon one fearful of affliction, to tell me what I am to hope for.[24]

The most remarkable assertion of love comes towards the end of the play, when giving up the pretence of madness, he says to Angelica:

> Nay Faith, now let us understand one another, Hypocrisie apart—The Comedy draws to an end and let us think of leaving acting, and be our own selves; and since you have lov'd me, you must own, I have at length deserv'd you should confess it.[25]

Later still, confronting his father he says:

> I have been disappointed of my only Hope; and he that loses Hope may part with anything...my only Pleasure is to Pleasure this lady.[26]

And now Angelica, giving up all pretence, confesses her love straight to him:

> Had I the World to give you, it cou'd not make me worthy of so generous and faithful a Passion: Here's my hand, my Heart was always yours and struggl'd very hard to make this utmost Trial of your Virtue.[27]

All these quotations from the text about the good-humoured tolerance and lack of satire in the play on one hand, and the depth and sincerity of love on the other have been necessary because Dobrée does not believe in either of these factors. He believes the play to be satirical both about man's nature and love. It is difficult to see how he can think so, specially about love as very few speeches about it have been quoted. There are many more protestations of love on the part of Valentine and

Angelica and while it is difficult to agree with Dobrée one has to justify the disagreement.

Dobrée does not have much praise about the play. First of all, he is of the opinion that it was the use of the characteristics of Ben Jonson's humour plays that had made the play so popular, but it is clear from his tone that he does not much approve of it:

> ...it was the return to a certain Jonsonian obviousness that made Love for Love so palatable to playgoers.[28]

Again, he is convinced that Congreve is far more satirical than he admits:

> (a) Indeed, Congreve from the first had not been altogether averse from satire and could make excellent thrusts, but his hand was too light for a whole "essay" in this kind.... It follows that many passages, though they are good Wycherley, are poor Congreve.
>
> (b) The satirical lash is again apparent in the famous Tattle-Prue scene.[29]

Again, speaking of Angelica, he neglects all the sentences of sincere love on her part and quotes some of her light-hearted, sportive sentences but has something positive to say about her character, though not about her love:

> This is not the observation of a jilt, of a baggage without sensibility but of a woman who has known and suffered, who has been disappointed in her early estimate of things.[30]

Then, speaking collectively of the first three plays, he makes an observation which is applicable to *Love for Love*:

> The thread of sadness and disillusion runs through these plays and live passions break through the veil of cynicism wherewith the critical comedy clothes itself.[31]

It can be seen thus that Dobrée judges the play to be much more satirical than Congreve says than, on reading, it appears to be.

Though Dobrée does not have much praise for this play, it was judged to be one of his best, surpassed only by *The Way of the World*. There are many reasons for this also. First of all, there are three songs in it. The first song is in III, iii. It is a light love-song, based on classical myth. Oddly enough, Cupid does not figure in it, but Apollo which one would hardly expect in a love-song. It is supposed to be a song from a contemporary play. The second song is quite a long ballad sung by Ben in III, xv. It is a typical love-song, simple in language and rhyming. The third song is more sophisticated, in IV, xvi, sung to the request of Valentine while he is pretending to be mad. The three songs increase its entertainment value considerably.

The play also contains many Senecan couplets, pinpointing the prevailing mood or moral of a scene or an Act. Thus, the first Act ends with one:

> Who hopes to purchase wealth by selling Land;
> Or win a mistress, with a losing Hand.[32]

Such couplets occur many more times and the one at the end, spoken by Angelica, is eloquent of her love.

Many quotations from the play have been given so far, but none to illustrate that fundamental ingredient in it, its wit. Indeed it is difficult to know which to choose. Thus, Tattle says to Prue:

> Besides, you are a Woman, you must never speak what you think: Your Words must contradict your Thoughts; but your Actions may contradict your Words.[33]

Angelica is a very lively and witty woman and says to Sir Sampson:

> If I marry, Sir Sampson, I'm for a good Estate with any Man, and for any Man with a good Estate.[34]

No list of wit can be complete without the famous lines by Valentine:

> My Friend, what to do? I am no married Man, and thou canst not lye with my wife: I am very poor, and thou canst borrow Money of me: Then what Employment have I for a friend?[35]

It can be seen that it is not for nothing that this is taken to be one of the best plays of Congreve.

References

1. Dobrée, B. *op. cit.*, p. 123.
2. The Dedication Comedies by Congreve. *The World's Classics*, O.U.P. London, 1951 pp. 336-37.
3. Dobrée, B. ed. *Comedies* by William Congreve, by World's Classics, O.U.P., London, 1951. Prologue to *The Old Bachelor*, p. 22. All quotations from Congreve will be from this text. It will be referred to as: Congreve.
4. Dobrée, *op. cit.*, p. 126.
5. *Ibid.*
6. *Ibid.*, p. 127.
7. Hirst, D.L. *op. cit.*, p. 28.
8. *Ibid.*, p. 29.
9. Congreve, pp. 25-26.
10. *Ibid.*, p. 48.
11. *Ibid.*, p. 36.
12. *Ibid.*, p. 119.
13. Dobrée, pp. 127-28.
14. *Ibid.*, p. 128.
15. *Ibid.*
16. *Ibid.*, p. 131.
17. Hirst, *op. cit.*, p. 30.
18. Congreve, I, i.
19. *Ibid.*, I, ii.
20. *Ibid.*, I, iv.
21. *Ibid.*, I, vi.
22. *Ibid.*, Prologue.
23. *Ibid.*
24. *Ibid.* IV, iii.
25. *Ibid.* IV, xviii.
26. *Ibid.* Scene the Last.
27. *Ibid.*
28. Dobrée, *op. cit.*, p. 132.
29. *Ibid.*, pp. 133-34.
30. *Ibid.*, p. 137.

31. *Ibid.*, p. 138.
32. Congreve, I, xv.
33. *Ibid.*, II, xi.
34. *Ibid.*, III, v.
35. *Ibid.*, IV, xvi.

3

A Brief Outline and the Genre

A BRIEF OUTLINE

It is often said that the story of the play is a bit confusing as there are too many intrigues. Mirabell is the true-wit of the play, a man of fashion who is in love with Millamant, a most charming lady. She has been compared often with Rosalind, because of the opportunities she offers to an actress. Mirabell, earlier, had an affair with Arabella Languish who is now Mrs. Fainall. Fainall is the villain. Arabella is also the daughter of Lady Wishfort who controls half of Millamant's fortune, who is her niece. Mrs. Fainall (Arabella) and Mirabell had been lovers earlier and she is married to Fainall now, but there is no conflict between her and Mirabell. They are good friends now.

If Millamant marries Mirabell without the consent of Lady Wishfort she stands to lose half of her fortune. Lady Wishfort is dead against her marriage because she has a grudge against Mirabell. He had, earlier, in order to conceal his love for Millamant, paid court to her. Mrs. Marwood, the villainess of the piece, had disclosed the truth to her—Mirabell's pretence and his love for Millamant. Lady Wishfort, at fifty-five, is a very foolish lady and wants very much to marry again.

Mirabell takes full advantage of these foolish hopes. He makes up the plot that he has a rich uncle, Sir Rowlands and makes his servant Waitwell to act this role. He makes this fictitious uncle pay court to Lady Wishfort, thinking that she will marry him. He will then threaten to expose her and thus make her agree to his marriage with Millamant. He makes Waitwell marry Foible, Lady Wishfort's maid, before he starts courting her for he does not want to compromise or harm her seriously.

Witwoud's half-brother, Sir Wilfull Witwoud comes from the country to pay court to Millament. Lady Wishfort wants this for Sir Wilfull is her nephew and if he marries Millamant she will not have to pay Millamant her money. Millamant does not like him at all and refuses to even take a walk with him. She is in love with Mirabell—truly sincerely in love. She cannot possibly like anyone else, let alone a fool.

Disguised as Sir Rowlands, Waitwell pays court to Lady Wishfort. She is elated at this, but Fainall and Mrs. Marwood have come to know the whole plan and reveal all. Lady Wishfort is mortified and gets Waitwell arrested to revenge herself.

Then Fainall thinks of a plan to ruin her. He is carrying on an affair with Mrs. Marwood in secret, but he accuses his wife of having an affair with Mirabell. He threatens Lady Wishfort that he will discredit her by exposing this affair unless she does two things. She will have to submit her own property to him for management and make over her daughter's (who is Fainall's wife) property in his name. She is facing certain ruin now and in order to save her, Millamant agree to marry Sir Wilfull.

Then Mirabell takes on the role of a *deus ex machina*. He brings a black box which has important documents signed by Mrs. Fainall before her marriage when she was Arabella Languish. In this document, she had made Mirabell the guardian of all her property. So, it becomes clear that neither Fainall nor Lady Wishfort has any hold over her.

Before bringing out the document Mirabell had already stipulated that Lady Wishfort should agree to his marriage with Millamant. Since she has been saved from utter ruin, she grudgingly agrees to this. Sir Wilfull now reveals that he does not want to marry Millamant as she loves Mirabell. Very generously he congratulates the two of them and decides to go on a world tour.

This is the story in brief, and it has got some of the best witty passages in Congreve. Specially unforgettable is a passage by Foible to Lady Wishfort:

> I warrant you, Madam, a little Art once made your picture like you; and now a little of the same art will make you like your picture. Your Picture must sit for you Madam.[1]

It is sentences like these that made Dr. Johnson say:

> His personages are a kind of intellectual gladiators, every sentence is to ward or strike.[2]

There will be many more opportunities to give examples of his wit, this is just one instance.

THE GENRE OF THE PLAY

From the very beginning there has been no doubt about the genre of the play (*The W.W.* from now on). Supporting quotations from different critics will be given later, but now it will be more expedient to give the opinion of Dr. Johnson who is the only critic to offer us the view that it is like a tragedy. While agreeing that it is primarily a comedy, he also gives the view that it functions like a tragedy. He does not have much to say about Congreve the dramatist, only a paragraph of half a page. But in this para, there are some sentences that are highly quotable and pregnant with meaning. The sentences will be given as the relevant topic is taken for discussion. Now it is the question of genre. About this Dr. Johnson says:

> His Comedies have, therefore, in some degree, the operation of tragedy; they surprise rather than divert, and raise admiration after than merriment.[3]

It can be seen here that Dr. Johnson is talking of tragedy from an entirely technical point of view. He mentions two points: (i) his comedies surprise the reader rather than entertain him and (ii) they excite admiration than merriment. He does not touch upon the topics of purgation or of pity and terror though the second point, by mentioning admiration in contrast with merriment, hints at it. The two effects or functions of comedy both point at entertainment of the light-hearted kind rather than at seriousness.

It is a great pity that he does not discuss or analyse or explain the points. Indeed he does not do that with any of his highly valuable sentences. As a matter of fact, he dismisses Congreve's plays in a few cursory sentences, his main preoccupation being the poems of Congreve.

Now, many of the critics consider *The W.W.* as a plain and simple comedy of manners. Two such opinions will be enough. D.L. Hirst is one of them:

> It remains, however, our most complete and subtle comedy of manners, and a remainder that essentially this genre begins where Shakespeare and his contemporaries end: with marriage.[4]

Here again there is scope for doubt and disagreement about the statement that this genre and with it *The W.W.* begin with marriage when it is palpable that they (like Shakespeare as alleged by Hirst) end with it and sometimes the marriages are implied, they do not actually take place. This is what happens in *The Old Bachelor*, whereas it is not even implied in *The Double Dealer*. It is implied all right in *The W.W.* for it is quite clear that Mirabell and Millamant are going to marry, though it does not actually take place. So this play, belying Hirst's claim, ends like a Shakespearean comedy with marriage rather than begins with it.

Another critic who agrees whole-heartedly with the view that it is a comedy of manners is C.T. Thomas. In the text of the *The W.W.* edited by him, he refers to the play throughout as a comedy of manners. It is true that in one place he equates it with artificial comedy but as he does not differentiate between the artificial comedy and the comedy of manners it can be taken for granted that the play according to him is a comedy of manners.

After these opinions come those critics who, while admitting that it is a comedy of manners, qualify it in some way or another. First of all, there is Dobrée. It has been already explained earlier that he classifies comedy into three kinds. Since all this has already been explained, here only the relevant points are being quoted:

(1) The vast bulk of comedy is of the "Critical Variety". It expresses the general feeling of the community for which another name is morality.

(2) The comedy of manners, then, was no exception to any other critical comedy.

(3) The thread of sadness and disillusion runs through these plays [of Congreve] and live passions break through the veil of Cynicism wherewith the critical comedy clothes itself.[5]

According to Dobrée, then the comedy of manners is a branch, or a variety, of critical comedy which has developed out of the Jonsonian comedy of humour. It contains cynicism, morality, disillusionment. But in Congreve's plays strong emotions manifest themselves; breaking through the veils of these essential elements of critical comedies. As, however, these points have been already discussed they are not being explained here. His point of view is quite clear.

Another important variation on the theme of the genre of these plays is the one given by Lamb, who calls them "Artificial Comedies". In one of the *Essays of Elia* entitled "On the Artificial Comedy of the Last Century", he writes about Restoration plays from a completely new point of view. D.L. Hirst puts it succinctly:

> His admiration for these dramas stems from his belief that the world they represent is unreal: "It is altogether a speculative scene of the things which has no reference whatever to the world that is."[6]

Lamb does not like the heavy morality of contemporary drama. It is most uninspiring, and he is happy to support the amoral tone of the artificial comedy. He says in his wonderful prose:

> I am glad for a season to take an air beyond the diocese of a strict conscience.[7]

He calls the plays artificial comedy but it is quite clear that he means restoration plays. The most valuable point in his argument is that of the world these plays deal with is (a) an artificial world and (b) not concerned with morality. Both are disputable points and have been argued about at length by later critics, specially by Macaulay.

Another critic to use the term artificial comedy with a little modification is Schelling who says:

> In William Congreve the artificial comedy of manners reached its height.[8]

He modifies the concept of artificial comedy a bit by saying that:

> Artificial comedy became less and less a transcript of life as successive playwrights accepted its conventions instead of observing afresh the life about them. Congreve's first comedy was written before he knew anything about actual fashionable life and his last reports as cynically, if more elaborately, precisely the same sorts of personages the same intrigues and situations. The comedy exhibits a total absence of any standard of rectitude or honour in any sense whatever of that misused word.[9]

That is to say he presents the artificial comedy as being (a) products of convention, (b) without realism, and (c) without morality. So here again we see that it is almost a new genre for him. Thus, within the concept of artificial comedy, we find several variations, the important ones being those of Lamb and Schelling.

The genre of the play, therefore, though there is not much scope, has been interpreted in three or four different ways. Dr. Johnson calls it like a tragedy in its functions, Dobrée a critical comedy, several critics agree that it is a simple comedy of manners, Lamb calls it artificial comedy and so does Schelling. This is quite impressive for a play as restricted in its mode and theme as *The W.W.* is.

References

1. Congreve, p. 382.
2. Dr. Johnson, *Lives of the English Poets*, Vol. II, O.U.P. London '75 rept., p. 30.
3. *Ibid.*
4. Hirst, D.L., *op. cit.*, p. 35.
5. Dobrée, *op. cit.*, 1-pp. 10-11, 2-pp. 35, 3-pp. 138.
6. Hirst, *op. cit.*, p. 48.
7. Quoted by Hirst, *ibid.*
8. Schelling, F., *English Drama*, S. Chand & Co., 1963, New Delhi, p. 266.
9. *Ibid.*, p. 268.

4

A Scene-wise Analysis

The particular text consulted here is Thomas C.T. Ed., *William Congreve: The Way of the World* (*The W.W.*, from now on), The MacMillan's annotated Classics, 1978 ed.

THE DEDICATION

The play has been dedicated to the Earl of Montague who was a well-known patron of the Arts and member of the Kit Kat Club. The Dedication contains some observations on comedy by Congreve for which it is important.

His extremely lenient attitude towards follies and vices is made clear in the Dedication itself. He is not at all satirical but extremely tolerant:

> Those characters which are meant to be ridiculous in most of our comedies are of fools so gross that, in my humble opinion, they should rather disturb than divert the well-natured and reflecting part of an audience; they are rather objects of charity rather than contempt, and instead of moving our mirth, they ought very often to excite our compassion.[1]

This is not the attitude of a satirist but that of a forgiving observer of humanity and will be repeated again in the Prologue. Then he distinguishes between Truewits and Witwouds, giving his reasons for creating them at all:

> This reflection moved me to design some characters who should appear ridiculous, not so much through a natural folly (which is incorrigible and therefore not proper for the stage) as through an affected wit, which, at the same time that it is affected, is also false.[2]

This is very significant because it contains several important ideas about characters: (i) he deliberately designed characters who affect wittiness, (ii) naturally foolish characters are not proper for the stage, and (iii) the characters who affect wit are not real wits, but theirs is a falsely assumed wit. Here again we find a very liberal attitude. He has many more things to say in the Dedication, but they are not very relevant at present.

PROLOGUE

In the Prologue, Congreve modestly writes about the main features of his plays and also subtly flatters the audience:

> He owns, with toil he wrote the following scenes
> But if they're naught ne'er spare him for his pains
> . . . .
> Some plot we think he has and some new thought,
> Some humour too, no farce—but that is a fault.
> Satire, he thinks, you ought not to expect;
> For so reformed a town who dares correct?
> To please this time has been his sole pretence:
> He'll not instruct, lest it should give offence.
> Should he by chance a knave or fraud expose,
> That hurts none here; sure here are none of those.[3]

This is a very good declaration. Not only does he invite criticism but also, he flatters his audience by saying there are no fools among them, that the town is a very polished one and that he is not going to preach to them, but intends to please them. It is modest as well as very good-humoured.

Act I

The scene is located at a Chocolate House which was a popular rendezvous at that time. Mirabell and Fainall have been playing cards. They finish playing and start to talk. The night before Mirabell and Millamant had quarrelled and all the ladies had got together and it had seemed to Mirabell that they were waiting to get rid of him. Then Fainall reveals the fact that the ladies had had their cabal-night last night. Cabal meeting means the meeting of a secret society. The word is made up of the initial letters of the names of the members of Charles II's Committee of

Foreign Affairs, namely Clifford, Arlington-Buckingham, Ashley and Lauderdale.

Through their talk, we come to know most of the vital facts: that Lady Wishfort is fifty-five years old and that she is very angry with Mirabell because, he, in order to conceal his love for Millamant had pretended to pay court to her. We also come to know that Waitwell and Foible are married. It is in this Act that we have that famous speech in which Mirabell describes his love for Millamant:

> I like her with all her faults; nay, like her for her faults. Her follies are so natural, or so artful, that they become her.... They are now grown as familiar to me as my own frailties: and in all probability, in a little time longer, I shall like them as well.[4]

This, indeed, is true love—there is no doubt about it.

After this very important speech we come to know that Sir Wilfull Witwoud has come to town and his relationship with Lady Wishfort and with Fainall. Then other characters come in and they all talk together. Witwoud and Petulant come and we have a very lively conversation. The latter are both characters about whom he had written in the Dedication when he talked about the difference between Truewits and Witwouds.

It is a long Act. In the edition of the text being used it is more than five hundred lines long. As a matter of fact, though, it is the shortest in the play. The whole of Act I is just one scene. That is the case with all the Acts, each is one long unbroken scene in this edition. It will be expedient to give a plan of the play here:

Act I – lines 529

Act II – lines 551

Act III – lines 701

Act IV – lines 629

Act V – lines 622

This feature will be discussed more in detail in the chapter on Plot (Chap. 8). Meanwhile let it be noticed that some of the wittiest passages in Congreve occur in this Act. Specially revealing are the speeches of the Witwouds. They are so witty that they could easily have been spoken by the Truewits of other dramatists. A few examples are quoted below. Thus, Witwoud says:

(1) A wit should no more be sincere than a woman constant; one argues a decay of parts, as t'other of beauty.

(2) Aye, aye, friendship with freedom is as dull as love without enjoyment, or wine without toasting.[5]

If this is how his fools talk then Pope is indeed justified in asking "Tell me if Congreve's fools are fools indeed?" This is how a truewit of other dramatists talks.

There is an air of consequence, and of deliberation about the attitude of the would-be wits ("see how clever I am") that is in marked contrast with that of the conversation between the truewits and this is the only way in which the former differ from the latter. This is how Mirabell and Fainall talk:

Fainall: ...'tis for the honour of England that all Europe should know we have block heads of all ages.

Mirabell: I wonder there is not an act of parliament to save the credit of the nation, and prohibit the exportation of fools.

F.: By no means; 'tis better as 'tis. 'Tis better to trade with a little loss, than to be quite eaten up with being overstocked.[6]

Here there is not the least impression of artificiality. The two of them are talking perfectly naturally. It is not that they are striving after effects. The wit that is there is perfectly natural. It is this natural quality that is lacking in the talk of the would-be wits, no one here is trying to impress anybody. This can be said to be the only way in which Congreve differentiates between his Truewits and Witwouds. This happens every time, in every scene and Act. We shall come across this feature repeatedly in each Act: no ostentation.

Act II

The scene is located at St. James's Park, a pleasant promenade of the time. Mrs. Fainall and Mrs. Marwood are talking. The subject of their talk is the attitude of lovers. Mrs. Fainall finds that men are insupportable at all times, whether they are in love or not and Mrs. Marwood says that anything is better than never to have loved or been loved. The two of them talk with a natural wit that is just like Congreve:

> Mrs. F.: Men are ever in extreme, either doting or averse. While they are lovers, if they have fire and sense, their jealousies are insupportable and when they cease to be lovers...they loathe...they meet us like the ghosts of what we were.
>
> Mrs. M.: True, 'tis an unhappy circumstance of life, that love should ever die before us; and that the man so outlive the lover.[7]

This is polished, elegant and witty, yet perfectly natural. There is no impression of the two of them talking to impress each other—they are just two friends talking intimately. After a bit more of talk they agree that they both loathe men. Then it becomes clear that Mrs. Marwood is in love with Mirabell, though she denies it strenuously. It also becomes clear that Mrs. Fainall also likes him very much, though she too denies it.

Then Fainall and Mirabell enter. Mr. and Mrs. Fainall address each other very lovingly and yet one gets the impression that it is all artificial. Then Mrs. Fainall and Mirabell talk apart and Mrs. Marwood and Fainall are left together and Fainall confides quite clearly that he would like to get rid of his wife and it also becomes clear that the two of them are lovers and Fainall suspects that Mrs. Marwood has been deceiving him and is actually in love with Mirabell. They quarrel for some time accusing each other of deception and finally Mrs. Marwood threatens to expose his falsity to his wife:

> By all my wrongs I'll do it. I'll publish to the world the injuries you have done me both in my fame and fortune! With both I trusted you, you bankrupt in honour, as indigent of wealth.[8]

Fainall does not hold back in being frank and accuses her also, and ends his speech thus:

> And wherefore did I marry but to make lawful prize of a rich widow's wealth and squandered it on love and you?[9]

After some more of mutual recrimination Mrs. Marwood is going to go away and then Fainall changes his front and wants to be reconciled to her. He tries his best to persuade her and promises to marry her. (She is unmarried. All women were called "Mrs." in those days.):

> I'll hate my wife yet more, damn her! I'll part with her, rob her of all she's worth, and we'll retire somewhere, anywhere, to another world. I'll marry thee, be pacified[10]

This presents a sorry picture of the society they live in. Congreve has no mercy at all on society, in general, however forgiving he might be of individuals.

Then Mirabell and Mrs. Fainall enter, and we find Mrs. Fainall telling Mirabell of her love for him. Here Mirabell emerges in no good light. It appears that he made Fainall marry her because he knew him to be a morally lax person. In this connection, he makes a long and revealing speech. It is a nearly 15 lines long speech and the characters of these plays do not usually deliver speeches so long. The tone of the speech is solemn rather than light-hearted and witty:

> Why do we daily commit disagreeable and dangerous actions? To save that idol, reputation. If the familiarities of our loves had produced that consequences of which you were apprehensive, where could you have fixed a father's name with credit but on a husband? I knew Fainall to be a man lavish of his morals, an interested and professing friend, a false and a designing lover.[11]

This speech reveals Mirabell's character as well as the society he lives in, where nothing is sacred, neither friendship, nor morality nor anything else. No wonder Coleridge made his famous remark about evil being not made for comedy with reference to Congreve's plays. It reveals Mirabell as an immoral opportunist.

More of the plot is revealed through their conversation, for example, the role Waitwell has to play, his marriage to Foible and the whole plan concerning them, in fact. It had not been so clearly explained before this. Here the audience is informed about the entire plan in detail. There are some remarkable observations about Lady Wishfort's craving after marriage which are often taken as typical examples of wit combined with wisdom and then Millamant comes in. She is ushered in by a much-quoted sentence of Mirabell:

> Here she comes, i'faith, full sail, with her fan spread and her streamers out, and a shoal of fools for tenders.[12]

This passage is so important that it deserves a few comments here. It has been compared with Milton's description of Delilah in Samson Agonistes:

> Comes this way sailing
> Like a stately ship
> . . . .
> With all her bravery on, and tackle trim,
> Sails fill'd, and streamers waving
> Courted by all the winds that hold them play.[13]

The resemblance is striking. It is also a Homeric simile.

Witwoud is with her and is inspired to give off witty remarks one after another, though Millamant says she is tired of them. There is a lot of sparkling dialogue among them all, even Mincing (Millamant's maid) bearing her part creditably. Then comes a famous dialogue between Mirabell and Millamant:

> Mir.: ...when you have lost your lover, your beauty dies upon the instant. For beauty is the lover's gift; it's he bestows your charms, your glass is all a cheat....
>
> Mill.: ...Beauty the lover's gift! Lord, what is a lover, that it can give? Why, one makes lovers as fast as one pleases, and they live as long as one pleases, and they die as soon as one pleases; and then, if one pleases, one makes more.[14]

There are hardly any other heroines who are more charming than Millamant. It is not for nothing that she has been compared with Rosalind. Both of them offer great opportunities to the actress. All that she says here is light-hearted bantering, not meant to be taken seriously, yet it is not that Mirabell does not take this persiflage as lightly as it is meant to be taken. It comes out into the open when he too talks wittily but with an underlying vein of seriousness clearly perceptible in his response. When Witwoud and Mrs. Fainall go out, he says to Millamant, accusing her of neglecting him the previous evening:

> You had the leisure to entertain a herd of fools; things who visit you from their excessive idleness, bestowing on your easiness that time which is the encumbrance of their lives. How can you find delight in such society? It is impossible they should admire you; they are not capable. Or if they were, it should be to you as a mortification, for sure to please a fool is some degree of folly.[15]

This is serious, Millamant continues her light-hearted-ness but he continues to be serious and she says:

> Mirabell, if you persist in this offensive freedom, you'll displease me.[16]

Yet Mirabell continues to be serious and is reproved. He says:

> I say that a man as soon make a friend by his wit, or a fortune by his honesty, as win a woman within plain dealing and sincerity.[17]

Millamant then chides him:

> Sententious Mirabell! Prithee, don't look with that violent and inflexible wise face, like Solomon at the dividing of the child in an old tapestry hanging.[18]

She then tells him that she knows of his plan about Waitwell and Foible and he wonders at her knowledge of it. Then she goes out to leave Mirabell talking to himself. There is again a long speech by him, of nearly 15 lines, full of metaphors and similes.

Then Waitwell and Foible enter, and Foible tells Mirabell that she has told Lady Wishfort about Sir Rowland and that he is eager to see her. We have witty talk from both of them. For example, Waitwell says:

Married, knighted and attended all in one day! 'Tis enough to make any man forget himself.[19]

This is an example of how Congreve endows all his characters with wit, whether a beau or a servant.

Act III

This is the middle Act of the play and the longest, consisting of 700 lines. It opens with Lady Wishfort at her toilet. She is the fifty-five-year old aunt of Millamant who controls half of her fortune and without her consent she cannot marry. Lady Wishfort herself is crazy to be married and Mirabell has arranged to introduce his servant Waitwell to her, disguised as his uncle Sir Rowland, to court her. The two previous Acts have already explained his plan to the audience and shown the beginnings of it in the marriage of Waitwell and Foible. Foible is Lady Wishfort's maid and Lady Wishfort, at her toilet, asks for her. She is a very ill-tempered and foolish woman and treats the woman waiting on her as dirt as she is angry with Foible for being absent. Mrs. Marwood then comes in and she tells her that she has seen Foible talking with Mirabell. At this Lady Wishfort gets very angry because she cannot bear him. He had pretended to court her in the past falsely to hide his love for Millamant from her.

Lady Wishfort asks Mrs. Marwood to go into the closet because she wants to cross-question Foible concerning Mirabell. Foible tells her that she has seen Sir Rowland and shown him her picture and he is already enamoured of her and wants to meet her. Lady Wishfort is elated and then asks Foible what has she told Mirabell. Foible manages to fob her off with a lot of lies and Lady Wishfort believes it all and decides to marry Sir Rowland and thus disinherit Mirabell as Sir Rowland is his uncle.

Then she asks Foible to put new make-up on her face before she meets Sir Rowland for she is looking absolutely ragged and here comes Foible's famous sentence:

> I warrant you, madam, a little art once made your picture like you; and now a little more of the same art must make you like your picture. Your picture must sit for you, madam.[20]

This is perhaps the most famous example of how Congreve endows his minor characters with wit.

In the ensuing dialogue between her and Lady Wishfort we see more examples of Lady Wishfort's foolishness. Then, after getting ready. She goes out and Mrs. Fainall enters. She tells Foible that she knows the whole plan. Thus, reassured, Foible tells her of the progress of Mirabell's plan so far. They then go out and Mrs. Marwood enters. She had been hiding in a closet near the room as Lady Wishfort had asked her and heard everything that had passed between Mrs. Fainall and Foible. In quite a long speech, she gives vent to her spleen, specially against Fainall.

Then Lady Wishfort enters. She had forgotten all about asking Mrs. Marwood hiding in the closet and has now remembered it and has come to ask her pardon. She is expecting her nephew, Sir Wilfull Witwoud to come and met her before setting out on his travels. Mrs. Marwood puts the idea of getting him to marry Millamant. While Lady Wishfort goes out to get ready, Millamant enters with Mincing, her maid. She had been with Witwoud and Petulant and is very annoyed as they started quarrelling. Here Mrs. Marwood expresses a piece of worldy-wiseness: a lady should encourage fools in order to mask her real love-affairs:

> For a fool's visit is always a disguise, and never admitted by a woman of wit, but to blind her affairs with a lover of sense.[21]

She further tells Millamant that the whole town knows that Mirabell and she love each other and implies that it is something disgraceful. Millamant openly says she is malicious and defies her. Then she pretends to make fun of Mirabell and laughs at him. Mrs. Marwood is not taken in by this pretence. Most maliciously she tells Millamant that her merriment might soon change and Millamant lightly says that she will have a song to raise her spirits and a song is sung accordingly. It is the first song in the play.

As soon as the song is finished Petulant and Witwoud enter. Millamant, who had been indignant with them asks them if their quarrel is over and they are most good-humouredly tell her that their quarrel was not serious:

> Raillery, Madam, raillery; we have no animosity.... The falling-out of wits is like the falling-out of lovers; we agree in the main, like treble and bass.[22]

There is some general talk among them for some time. Then Millamant, seeing other people coming, leaves.

The person she had seen coming was Sir Wilfull Witwoud who had come to dine with Lady Wishfort. He is a country gentleman and is going to set out in a world tour to improve his mind. Before setting out on this long journey he has come to meet her because he is her nephew. He is also Witwoud's half-brother. He is dressed like a country squire and that surprises Witwoud so much that he does not recognize him at first. He would naturally look out-of-place among all these elegantly dressed men-about-town but that does not necessarily mean that he is a fool. Indeed, in his subsequent behaviour he proves himself to be a sensible man. But all that comes later. Just now a servant of Lady Wishfort accompanies him and it becomes clear that Lady Wishfort cannot keep her servants.

Then Sir Wilfull greets those who are present on the stage (Petulant, Witwoud and others) and they tease him, trying to make him feel like a country bumpkin, but he holds his own and after some time, Lady Wishfort and Fainall come in. She welcomes him. Then dinner is announced. So everyone goes out except Mrs. Marwood and Fainall. The latter talks about Foible's duplicity and for the first time the name of the play is used:

> And I, it seems, am a husband, a rank husband; and my wife a very arrant, rank wife, all in the way of the world.[23]

He has now discovered that Mirabell has made a fool of him. In the last Act, he had clarified that he had deliberately made him marry Mrs. Fainall, though at that time he himself was having an affair with her. He had done so quite deliberately in order to give his mistress's child a father's name because Fainall was a dishonourable man (page 40 of the text). He very much resents the fact that Mirabell has made a cuckold of him.

Mrs. Marwood and he then plan how to use the situation to their advantage. Mrs. Marwood tells him to tell Lady Wishfort of her daughter's (Mrs. Fainall) conduct and threaten to expose her. This will ruin her, and she will be ready to do anything to save herself and her daughter. They both plan it out in detail and Fainall ends the scene with a Senecan couplet:

> All husbands must or pain or shame endure
> The wise too jealous are, fools too secure.[24]

This couplet ably sums up the lesson he has learnt, and wants to convey. So now the plot has taken shape, with Lady Wishfort's ruined plan. Thus, Act III, the longest Act in the play, comes to an end.

Act IV

This Act is the one that contains the famous Bargaining scene. But that comes a little later and the scene starts with Lady Wishfort making things ready for the reception of Sir Rowland. Then after being reassured by Foible that everything is ready she starts worrying about herself: how she is looking, how she should receive him, etc., as though she were a young girl instead of a woman who has left the middle age behind her and is verging on old age. Then she arranges for Foible to call her when Sir Wilfull is paying court to Millamant as she had directed him to do and goes out.

Then Millamant and Mrs. Fainall come in and Foible tells Millamant that Mirabell has been waiting to talk to her. She walks about, reciting a poem by Sir John Suckling to herself. Sir Wilfull comes and Mrs. Fainall talks to him as Millamant had asked her to. While she is still reciting Suckling to herself Sir Wilfull tries to court her and asks her to come for a walk with him and she refuses. She asks to be excused by him and shows him the way out of the room.

Then she recites a line from a poem by Waller, and Mirabell comes in to supply the next line. Here the Bargaining scene starts. Millamant is at her most charming in this scene. She says to Mirabell that she wants to be pursued to the last. But there is some cause for elation on Mirabell's part because she seems to have accepted his courtship of her whereas formerly, she used to speak to the contrary. Now she says:

> Though I am upon the very verge of matrimony I expect you should solicit me as much as if I were wavering at the grate of a monastery, with one foot over the threshold. I'll be solicited to the very last, nay, and afterwards.[25]

There are many more of these conditions she lays down. She says:

> Oh, I hate a lover that can dare to think he draws a moment's air independent on the bounty of his mistress.... Ah, I will never marry, unless I am first made sure of my will and power.[26]

Mirabell is not behindhand either. He gives as good as he takes:

> Will you have 'em both before marriage?
>
> Or will you be contented with the first now, and stay for the other till after grave?[27]

There are many more of such charming conditions. Then Mirabell puts his own conditions. It is a Bargaining scene after all, so why should not be put his own conditions as well?

> I article that you continue to like
> your own face as long as I shall, and
> while it passes currency with me that
> you endeavour not to new-coin it.[28]

Then, after some time he lays down the condition that when she is pregnant she will not do any strait-lacing, i.e. wear tight corsets. He lays down some more conditions and after some time Mrs. Fainall comes and the Bargaining scene comes to an end. Mrs. Fainall tells her to have him as she is sure she wants him and Millamant says:

> Are you? I think I have—and the horrid man looks as if he thought so too—Well, you ridiculous thing you, I'll have you.[29]

It will be seen that while her conditions are charming trifles, his are all serious ones—that she should not have any close confidants, go to the plays with males while wearing a mask, paint her face, not use corsets when pregnant and when in that condition confine herself to a limited diet, i.e., for tea, drink only tea, chocolate and coffee (not have beer or brandy, etc.). They are both deeply in love with each other. The Bargaining scene is a playful proposal scene. Both of them, behind the light talk, are entirely serious.

So now their marriage, as far as they themselves are concerned is a settled thing, but so far only Mrs. Fainall knows about it. Meanwhile, she tells him to go backstairs where Foible is waiting to speak to him. There is one more avowal of love from Millamant. She says to Mrs. Fainall:

> Well, if Mirabell should not made a good husband I am a lost thing—for I find I love him violently.[30]

Then one by one the men enter, Witwoud and Petulant, and both of them are drunk. The two of them talk and after some time, Lady Wishfort and Sir Wilfull enter, the latter drunk. Lady Wishfort is angry with him as she wants him to court Millamant and he is in a drunken condition. He does not care for her anger and sings and talks drunkenly. Quite disgusted, Millamant and Mrs. Fainall go out. He still goes on singing and Foible comes and tells Lady Wishfort that Sir Rowland is getting impatient. Then all three of them go out and Waitwell, disguised as Sir Rowland, enters.

Waitwell pays court to her most efficiently and both of them talk about Mirabell. Then Foible comes and says there is someone with a letter for Lady Wishfort. While she is reading it there is a dance and Foible sees that the letter is from Mrs. Marwood. She tells Waitwell to do something about it and he quickly says to Lady Wishfort that the letter is not written by a woman but by a man. Waitwell somehow persuades her that it is by Mirabell, that he is hatching a plot against her. She believes him implicitly and they decide that they will get married that very night in order to ruin him.

Here this Act ends. The most important thing in it is the Bargaining scene. But besides that, one can see that the plot has progressed substantially in it. Lady Wishfort and Waitwell are as good as married and the plot against Mirabell has progressed so much that his downfall seems to be imminent. On the other hand, from Mirabell's point of view, he is engaged to Millamant and his plot against Lady Wishfort with Waitwell and Foible is also proceeding successfully till Lady Wishfort's fall or capitulation seems to be certain. The last Act will show us who wins.

The Act contains songs and dances, i.e. the element of spectacle, one of the Aristotelian requirements, so its entertainment value is considerable, and it ends with a Senecan couplet that sums up Waitwell's role in the play.

Act V

This Act is located, like the last, in Lady Wishfort's house and it opens with a scene of violence. Lady Wishfort is furious with Foible and is driving her out of the house. Foible tries to save herself by saying that Mirabell had promised that she (Lady Wishfort) will come to no harm at all if Foible did as he told her to do. The mention of Mirabell angers Lady Wishfort all the more. Then Foible tells her that Waitwell could not have married her because he was married to Foible first. Lady Wishfort shouts at her that Waitwell is already in prison and she too will soon be under arrest and goes out.

Mrs. Fainall comes and Foible tells her that she is going to be put under custody soon. Mrs. Fainall tells her not to despair, that Mirabell has already gone to give security for Waitwell and tells her that this is the work of her husband and Mrs. Marwood. Then Foible tells her how villainous she is. After some more talk about the villainy of the two Foible gives her an important bit of news—that the two of them are lovers. Both she and Mincing (who is Millamant's maid) know about it. While they are still talking, Mincing herself comes and says Millamant is waiting to talk to Foible. Mirabell has set Waitwell free. She also tells them that Lady Wishfort is very disturbed at something Fainall has said. Mincing also gives them the news that she has been sent to bring Sir Wilfull to them.

Events are speeding up. Mincing and Foible go out and Lady Wishfort and Marwood enter. Lady Wishfort is extremely grateful to Mrs. Marwood for having disclosed the plot about Waitwell to her. She turns to Mrs. Fainall and accuses her of ruining her and Mrs. Fainall in turn accuses Mrs. Marwood of complicity with Fainall. While her mother is still blaming her, she defies them and goes out. As it is, Lady Wishfort is a credulous fool and she still goes on lamenting and pleading with Mrs. Marwood not to desert her. There is a long dialogue between them.

Then Fainall enters. He pretends to have been persuaded by Mrs. Marwood to relent towards Lady Wishfort, allowing her to keep her property to herself on condition that she promises never to marry, and he also wants the six thousand pounds which is Millamant's property.

Then he goes out and Millamant and Sir Wilfull enter. The latter tells her that he is ready to marry Millament and Millamant tells her that in order to save her from ruin she is ready to make this sacrifice and Mirabell is ready to give up his claims on her. He and Sir Wilfull are going to travel together. He brings Mirabell in and Mirabell speaks most eloquently to her:

> I come not to plead for favours; nay, nor for pardon. I am a supplicant only for your pity. I am going where I never shall behold you more.[31]

He has brought a document in which he gives up all claims on Millamant in writing and just then Fainall and Mrs. Marwood also enter, Fainall bringing a document for Lady Wishfort's signing. She tells him that she cannot sign it because Millamant is already engaged to Sir Wilfull. Nothing moves him. He is determined to expose her daughter's misdeeds and in order to save her, Lady Wishfort must sign his paper, agreeing to all his conditions.

While she is lamenting Mirabell steps in. He says he has a means of saving her, if she will accept it. He cannot bear to see her "wronged in this savage manner" as he puts it. Then he brings in his witnesses and culprits. First of all, enter Mrs. Fainall, Foible and Mincing. They are to bear witness. Seeing them, Fainall realizes that the game is up but he is still the villain he was—he is not going to give up his claim. He says in a speech, using the name of the play:

> If it must all come out, why let 'em know it; 'tis but the way of the world. That shall not urge me to relinquish or abate one title of my terms. No, I will insist the more.[32]

Foible and Mincing both bear solemn witness to his villainy and Lady Wishfort is at last convinced:

> O Marwood, Marwood, art thou false? my friend deceive me? Hast thou been a wicked accomplice with that profligate man?[33]

Fainall, however, still stands firm on his villainy:

> Well, what are you the better for this?
> Is this Mr. Mirabell's expedient?
> I'll be put off no longer. You thing, that was
> a wife, shall smart for this: I will not leave thee
> wherewithal to hide thy shame; your body shall be
> as naked as your reputation.[34]

This is truly wicked, specially the vindictiveness against his wife. No wonder Coleridge had made his famous remark about wickedness with reference to Congreve:

> Wickedness is no subject for comedy. This was Congreve's great error and peculiar to him. The dramatic personalities of Dryden, Wycherley and others are often viciously indecent, but not like Congreve's, wicked.[35]

This does not yet solve Lady Wishfort's problem. Then Waitwell appears with a box full of papers. This is the famous black box that solve all problems, carrying out the function of *deus ex machina*. It is not very correct to call the box the *deus ex machina*, for actually it belongs to Mirabell.

Then Petulant and Witwoud come in. In this last part of the play, all the characters have to be present. So these two also come, but not just to fill the stage. They have to bear witness. Mirabell wants them to affirm that they had signed a certain parchment and they do so. In a substantial speech Mirabell, holding up that paper and displaying it to all, says that Mrs. Fainall, before she was married, had left all her property to Mirabell in trust. Fainall reads aloud:

> A deed of conveyance of the whole estate real of Arabella Languish, widow, in trust to Edward Mirabell.[36]

Now he is utterly defeated and Mirabell cannot help a crow of triumph; using the name of the play for the third time he says:

> Even so, sir, 'tis the way of the world, sir, of the widows of the world. I suppose this deed may bear an elder date than what you have obtained from your lady.[37]

Fainall, losing his control over himself, tries to attack Mrs. Fainall and Sir Wilfull holds him back.

Lady Wishfort, then, performs her part according to the promise she had made to Mirabell:

> Well, Mr. Mirabell, you have kept your promise and I must perform mine. First, I pardon, for your sake, Sir Rowland there and Foible.[38]

The next step is to tell Sir Wilfull that now that the problem is solved, she is obliged to give Millamant to Mirabell and therefore he cannot marry her. It is an embarrassing position for her and she hesitates. Then Mirabell tells her not to worry. Sir Wilfull is his friend, and he has compassion upon lovers. Sir Wilfull supports him and says he has no mind to marry. He will set forth on his travels and he asks Witwoud and Petulant to come with him. He shows himself as a generous and sensible person.

Lady Wishfort then tells Mirabell to take Millamant. A lovely passage follows:

> Mill.: Why does not the man take me?
>
> Would you have me give myself over to you again?
>
> Mir: Aye, and over and over again; for I would have you, as often as I possibly can.[39]

Then there is a dance and after that in front of everyone Mirabell restores the deed of trust to Mrs. Fainall so that she may live comfortably hereafter. Then he ends the play with two Senecan couplets:

> From hence let those be warned, who mean to wed,
> Let mutual falsehood stain the bridal bed;
> For each deceiver to his cost may find,
> That no marriage frauds too oft are paid in kind.[40]

THE EPILOGUE

In the Epilogue, Congreve divides the playgoers into several classes, i.e., those who go to criticise, those who go to find who are the persons who have been copied or satirised, etc. In addition, he shows his high opinion of satire:

> For well the learned and the judicious know
> That satire scorns to stoop so meanly low
> As any one abstracted fop to show.[41]

Besides these lines, the Epilogue does not contain any very serious views on satire or on drama.

References

1. *The Dedication,* p. 3.
2. *Ibid.*
3. *Prologue*, pp. 7-8.
4. I, p. 15, ll. 154-71.
5. I, p. 1, ll. p. 22.
6. I, p. 16, ll. 194-202.
7. II, p. 30. ll. 3-12.
8. II, p. 37, ll. 191-94.
9. II, p. 38, ll. 203-05.
10. II, p. 39, ll. 240-43.
11. II, p. 40, ll. 199-266.
12. II, p. 42, ll. 317-18.
13. Bush, D. ed. *Milton's Poetical Works*, O.U.P. '79, p. 535, ll. 713-19.
14. II, p. 45, ll. 384-398.
15. II, p. 46, ll. 423-430.
16. II, p. 47, ll. 438-39.
17. II, p. 47, ll. 454-56.
18. II, p. 47, ll. 454-59.
19. II, p. 51, ll. 541-42.
20. III, p. 57, ll. 147-50.
21. III, p. 62, ll. 301-304.
22. III, p. 65, ll. 380-83.
23. III, p. 74, ll. 605-07.
24. III, p. 77, ll. 700-01.
25. IV, p. 84, ll. 151-55.
26. IV, p. 84, ll. 165-72.

27. IV, p. 84, ll. 172-75.
28. IV, p. 86, ll. 240-42.
29. IV, p. 88, ll. 288-90.
30. IV, p. 89, ll. 310-11.
31. p. 114, ll. 377-79.
32. V, p. 118, ll. 476-79.
33. V, p. 118, ll. 482-84.
34. V, p. 119, ll. 494-99.
35. Quoted in Dobrée, *op. cit.* p. 122.
36. V, p. 121, ll. 551-53.
37. V, p. 121, ll. 554-56.
38. V, p. 122, ll. 570-72.
39. V, p. 123, ll. 592-95.
40. V, p. 124, ll. 619-20.
41. Epilogue, ll. 29-31.

5

The Major Themes

Critics think that the theme of the play is love. Bonamy Dobrée however thinks differently: that the theme is the creation of beauty through words. Another opinion is that legacy-hunting is the theme. All of these should be examined.

THE THEME OF LOVE

This theme is present everywhere in these plays. Literary critics mostly think that in these comedies love has been presented in an unidealized and entirely cynical way. This is why Thackeray has called it "that banquet of wit where no love is." Many critics, however, take a more positive view, including Dobrée. He thinks that the essential Congreve, the true Congreve is seen in his treatment of this theme. Naturally, therefore, he lays stress upon the love between Mirabell and Millamant. One must remember, however, that different kinds and degrees of love are there in the play and the love between these two is of the very noblest thing—true and enduring, sincere love.

Certain other kinds of love, however, have to be mentioned before we turn to that love. The love between Mirabell and Mrs. Fainall in the past has, however, reached the stage of pure friendliness. Mrs. Marwood, too, feels attracted to Mirabell, then she unites with Fainall to whom also she is attached with love and also for gain. Fainall has married his wife for her wealth, and yet is jealous when he thinks of her in love with Mirabell though it is not true. These attachments and attractions, however, are of so inferior a kind that they can hardly be called love.

Turning to Mirabell and Millamant, here we have true love indeed—glorious true love in the traditional sense. The Bargaining scene is light-hearted and witty, but all the arguments in it cannot hide the depth of this love. Dobrée calls this wonderful scene "Congreve's contribution to the philosophy of love". This is the true love that serious poetry celebrates. After the Bargaining scene, Millamant, who has been frivolous all along, becomes serious and says to Mrs. Fainall:

> Well, if Mirabell should not make a good husband, I am a lost thing—for I find I love him violently.[1]

Mirabell had expressed his lovelorn condition in the very beginning to Fainall:

> I like her with all her faults; nay, like her for her faults. Her follies are so natural, or so artful, that they become her.[2]

Though the expression is light, this is Congreve's equivalent of Romeo's exclamation "O she doth teach the torches to burn bright!" This makes Lamb's Utopia of gallantry and Thackeray's "banquet of wit where no love is" sound hollow and false.

Thus, does Congreve express what Dobrée calls his "philosophy of love" through the many relationships in the play? When in the Prologue he had said:

> Some Plot we think he has, and some new Thought perhaps

he had meant this serious treatment of the theme of love in this play.

THE THEME OF BEAUTY

Dobrée thinks that it is the creation of beauty through words that is the theme of the play, like that of a poet, or as in Flaubert. In *The W.W.*, he had reached his aim:

> All the time, behind the coldly critical surface, there is much of the poet, of the man hungry for beauty. There is often a caressing touch, and Millamant he must really have loved.[3]

He had a dislike of human folly, and he wanted to convey positive values, but above it all was the desire for "creation of beauty by plastic means", that is, through the use of words. He did not say it openly and clearly, but in the Dedication he wrote repeatedly of "purity of style" and "perfection of dialogue". This explains the fact why his dialogue is so brilliant and even his would-be wits speak like truewits. Meredith's well-known passage becomes specially relevant:

> He hits the mean of the fine style and a natural dialogue. He is at once precise and valuable.... In this he is a classic, and is worthy of treading a measure with Molière.[4]

Almost the same thing has been said of Shakespeare's poetry in *Antony and Cleopatra* by Bradley. Actually, however, this comes under the topic of style and should be dealt with under that heading.

The Theme of Legacy-hunting

Paul Mueschke thinks that the whole play is built around the theme of legacy conflicts. He says that this is the main theme of the play.

The theme of inheriting or that of disinheriting dominates the whole play. Right at the beginning, in the very first scene, it is mentioned in connection with Millamant as half of her fortune is under Lady Wishfort's control and she must have her consent for her marriage:

> What? though half her fortune depends
> upon her marrying with my Lady's approbation?[5]

In the same Act, this theme is mentioned once again. As Petulant comes in he mentions that Mirabell's uncle has come to town. If he marries and has a son it will disinherit Mirabell. Later, of course, the reader comes to know that it is all just a fiction, as it is Waitwell who disguises himself as his uncle, but it is important for Lady Wishfort.

Thus, we find the theme of inheritance or disinheritance dominating the play. Fainall had married Lady Wishfort's daughter only because then he would get all her money:

> And wherefore did I marry but to make lawful prize of a rich widow's wealth and squander it on love and you?[6]

After frittering away all her money, he makes up plans for getting all of Lady Wishfort's money by threatening to expose her supposed adultery and divorcing her. Lady Wishfort plans to deprive Mirabell of his inheritance by marrying his supposed uncle, who is actually Waitwell, Mirabell's servant. The situation is saved at the last moment by the papers in the black box that providentially make Mirabell the trustee of all the property of Mrs. Fainall. Thus, the legacy-hunting theme, as it is apparent, is one that is there from the beginning along with the theme of love and manipulates the action.

While pointing out the difference between the comedy of humour and Restoration comedy, Bonamy Dobrée had said that the former is much more serious than the latter. For example in Ben Jonson's *Volpone* too legacy-hunting is the main theme and the difference can easily be seen if it is compared with *The Way of the World. Volpone* treats the theme so seriously that the play trembles on the verge of being a tragedy which is not the case with *The W.W.*—a light-hearted comedy.

References

1. IV, p. 89, ll. 310-11.
2. I, p. 15, ll. 155-57.
3. Dobrée, *op. cit.,* p. 125.
4. *Ibid.*, p. 122.
5. I, p. ii, ll. 45-46.
6. II, p. 38, ll. 203-05.

6
The Major Characters

In temperament and in action, Congreve's characters are partly like the Restoration dramatic characters. It is in their dialogue that they are different. But the main characters, specially Mirabell and Millamant, need separate study. His fools and Witwouds are far too witty to be like the ordinary characters. When critics talk about his characters, they talk more about their wit than about the traits of their personalities. Few indeed, are those who can separate the two. Dr. Johnson could and with his usual perspicacity said:

> ...his characters are commonly fictitious and artificial, with very little of nature and not much of life.[1]

Another such critic is Voltaire. He said that his "characters are shadowed with the utmost delicacy." His male characters, that is, are not all heartless beaux and his women heartless jilts. It was Allardyce Nicoll who said that his world is "a refinement, not a copy, of reality." In *The W.W.*, the only true villain is Fainall who hides the heart of a black conspirator behind his mask of friendship. Mrs. Marwood is definitely the villainess of the piece. But she secretly loves Mirabell, though she conspires with Fainall against him. This is exactly what Voltaire had meant when he talked about delicate shadowing of characters. This is a true description of minor characters, because individualization is necessary.

Dobrée has much to say about individual characters but does not pronounce anything about his characterization in general. Whenever he deals with characters he is preoccupied with wit and poetic beauty. For example, he remarks about the characters of *The Double Dealer*:

> These are not mere puppets, but breathing, living, desiring men and women.[2]

But this is not said about all the characters, only about those in *The Double Dealer*. About the art of characterization in *The W.W.*, he is of the opinion that it is much too serious for comedy:

> ...in many passages Congreve had ceased to write ordinary comedy. Whereas his secondary characters in previous plays...are made of that flimsy material which could enable Lamb to call them creatures of a sportive fancy, this is not the case with Mrs. Marwood and the Fainalls in this play.[3]

This is what Dobrée says about the characters in *The W.W.* C.T. Thomas, on the other hand, is of a different opinion. According to him, characterization in *The W.W.* is of a very delicate nature:

> Congreve's characterization in *The W.W.* is extremely subtle and delicate. His greatest creations are multi-dimensional.[4]

He illustrates this second valuable feature by taking Millamant as an example. According to him, she is "many-faceted, perfectly rounded picture" who is a combination of "sense and sensibility" both. Congreve has not idealized her, and she is fully realistic. But setting Millamant apart, almost every character in the play is multi-dimensional. We see many aspects of their personality in the play. Even the villainess Mrs. Marwood shows a completely different aspect of herself when she is with Fainall and cries so that Fainall has a tough time pacifying her.

Mirabell

Mirabell has received extravagant praise from critics. Meredith says he is "the sprightliest male figure of English Comedy." This implies a comparison not only with Restoration heroes, but with Elizabethan and Jacobean ones also, he is still the liveliest. Other critics have also waxed eloquent about his wit. W. Myers takes a more serious view as he thinks that the humanizing effect of the play depends largely on his insight into the minds of others. He can understand them and can act accordingly. He knows Petulant's inquisitive nature and when he hears that he has come to know about his imaginary uncle he questions him closely and is convinced that he will spread the news as he wants it to be spread. He makes Waitwell pretend to be Sir Rowland as he knows that he will be able to do it. The very fact he makes this plot proves he knows Lady Wishfort very well. He knows her weakness for marriage and the result shows how right he is as Lady Wishfort is mad to marry Sir Rowland though she is verging on old age.

> His love for Millamant is not a light hearted, casual affair as becomes clear when he tells Fainall.
>
> I like her with all her faults; nay, like her for her faults. Her follies are so natural, or so artful, that they become her.[5]

His clear-headedness as well as the intensity of his love are proved in the Bargaining Scene.

It is difficult to give examples of his wit as it is present everywhere. His famous description of the first appearance of Millamant is poetic:

> Here she comes i'faith full sail, with her fan spread and streamers out, and a shoal of fools for tenders.[6]

Apart from such lyrical outbursts, he quite often speaks in a way that combines poetry with awareness of the truth of real life. Describing Lady Wishfort's craze for marriage, he says:

> 'Tis the green-sickness of a second childhood; and like the fruit offering of a latter spring, serves but to usher in the Fall; and withers in an affected bloom.[7]

This is not just wit, but actually far more. Here his insight into human nature mingles with a poetic image of nature. This is like poetry, not prose.

He takes on the function of the *deus ex machina* by punishing Fainall and Mrs. Marwood at the end of the play, though he is not a god or even a person of authority like a king or a judge. It is not easy for an ordinary person to maintain such a role. It is, however, done superbly by him, without becoming sententious or unnaturally solemn or unbecomingly light-hearted. He strikes the golden mean. He makes the remark with the name of the play which preserves the light-hearted character of a Restoration comedy, or otherwise the play would have become much too solemn for one:

> Even so, Sir, 'tis the way of the world, Sir, of the widows of the world.[8]

Such is his sprightliness and charm that even the role of the *deus ex machina* sits lightly on him.

Millamant

Such is Millamant's infinite charm and grace that all the critics wax lyrical when talking about her. Actresses all want this role. Hazlitt and Meredith say about her:

> Hazlitt: She is the ideal heroine of the comedy. Wit is the habitual language she hears and speaks.
>
> Meredith: An air of bewitching whimsicality hovers over the graces of this comic heroine.

Love-letters in poetry serve to pin up her hair, for those in prose are not good enough. One of her best-known sayings is:

> Beauty the lover's gift—Lord, what is a lover, that it can give? Why, one makes lovers as fast as one pleases, and they live as long as one pleases, and they die as soon as one pleases; and then if one pleases, one makes more.[9]

She is, however, not as frivolous as this may seem to make her. She is a woman who makes Mirabell almost crazy with her whims and at the end of the Bargaining Scene she says to Mrs. Fainall:

> Well, if Mirabell should not make a good husband, I am a lost thing: for I find I love him violently.[10]

This, yet, does not display to the full the depth of her character. This can be understood when to save her aunt from being utterly ruined she agrees to marry Sir Willful whom before this she had called "Rusticke, ruder than Gothick", and had refused even to go for a stroll with. But when she comes to know that Fainall is going to ruin Lady Wishfort, she is ready to sacrifice her happiness and marry him. When at the end, all problems are solved, she restores the light-hearted touch of a comedy by saying to Mirabell:

> Why does not the man take me? Would you have me give myself to you over again?[11]

This is the note on which the play ends: of sincere, true love surrendering itself willingly but light-heartedly. This light, frivolous attitude cannot mask the depth of love, but it is necessary, for that is the characteristic attitude of true Restoration comedy. It remains for Millamant to recover this light touch for the scene up till then had been trembling on the verge of tragedy very much like Ben Jonson's *Volpone*. Yet it should be kept in mind that, if necessary, she can be serious also. Thus, she announces her decision to marry Sir Wilfull in quite a serious manner:

> I am content to be a sacrifice to your repose, madam and to convince you that I had no hand in this plot...I give my hand to this flower of knighthood.[12]

Such a speech proves that she can be firm and serious when needed. Moreover, we also have a glimpse here of a possible Millamant of the future for we can guess at what would have happened had she truly married the "flower of knighthood". We can be more or less sure that she would have treated him with all the honour due to him. She would have been faithful to him, though it would have broken her heart to have parted from Mirabell forever. She would have become a changed woman. Perhaps all her light-heartedness would have gone from her, perhaps she would have become a somber woman. But the fact is that we can envision this possibility and the very fact that we can do so is an indication of the multi-dimensionality that C.T. Thomas talks of. It is a clear indication of Congreve's mastery in the delicate shadowing that Voltaire too had mentioned.

The Humour Characters

It might seem strange that Congreve, who is a master of finesse, should depict beings like humour characters but there are no less than three such, Lady Wishfort, Sir Willful Witwoud and Petulant. They like all such characters, have names that clarify their natures. Lady Wishfort is the one who deserves some attention. Sir Wilfull has been treated gently, he is a country gentleman, rather stupid, no match for the wits. But he is neither punished nor reformed. He willingly resigns Millamant to Mirabell and decides to set out on his travels. He is really treated with velvet gloves, neither punished nor reformed at the end as is the fate of all such characters. Same is the case with Petulant.

Though a humour character, Lady Wishfort is delineated so strongly that she stands out even among the other characters. She is an elderly woman, as she is on the other side of fifty, but she is still frivolous, vain and absolutely crazy for marriage. She has not grown mature with age; it has not made any difference to her. It has rather, made her ridiculous instead of giving her dignity and maturity. Her language is polished and witty but Congreve has depicted her faults absolutely without pity:

> I shall die with confusion, if I am forced to advance.—Oh no, I can never advance—I shall swoon if he should expect advances.[13]

The attitude with which she receives the announcement that Millamant will marry Sir Wilfull is absolutely unforgiveable. She does not evince any love for her niece:

> Well, I'll swear I am something revived at this testimony of your obedience.[14]

And that is all from her. There is no whiff of gratitude. Congreve has not given her any virtues to tone down her selfishness.

References

1. *Op. cit.*, p. 30.
2. Dobrée, *op. cit.*, p. 137.
3. *Ibid.*
4. *Op. cit.*, p. 137.
5. I, p. 15, ll. 155-57.
6. II, p. 42, ll. 318-19.
7. II, 42, ll. 313-15.
8. V, p. 121, ll. 354-55.
9. II, p. 45, ll. 394-98.
10. IV, p. 89, ll. 310-11.
11. V, p. 123, ll. 592-93.
12. V, p. 113, ll. 329-33.
13. III, p. 57, ll, 154-57.
14. V, p. 113, ll. 338-39.

7

The Plot

Critics do not think unanimously about the plot or, in other words, the dramatic strategies of *The W.W.*, at all. Some think that there is no well-thought-out plot in the play and some think the opposite—that the plot is a carefully made one. This is largely because of Congreve's own attitude itself. He was an admirer of and was influenced by three dramatists all of whom were well known for their plots: Terence, Ben Jonson and Molière. They were all master craftsmen. Moreover, he has given the play a Prologue and an Epilogue in the classical manner, which means he had the conventional, classical structure in mind and framed his plays accordingly. He says in the Prologue, "Some plot we think he has". All this has made the critics think that the play has a neat structure.

It will be expedient to give here a short synopsis of the play Act by Act. First of all, it should be kept in mind that in the text that is being used all the Acts are one long scene without any scene-divisions.

Prologue – He says "some plot we think he has" but does not write anything more.

Act I – Mirabell's plan to discomfit Lady Wishfort mentioned. Waitwell and Foible married as part of it.

Act II – Mrs. Marwood's and Fainall's villainy explained. Fainall's duplicity in marrying Mrs. Fainall is explained.

Act III – Lady Wishfort determines to marry Sir Rowland. Fainall discovers that his wife had cuckolded him. Sir Wilfull Witwoud arrives.

Act IV – The Bargaining Scene in which Mirabell's marriage with Millamant is settled, Waitwell courts Lady Wishfort.

Act V – Fainall threatens Lady Wishfort with exposure of her daughter's adultery and imposes conditions to get all her property. Millamant agrees to marry Sir Wilfull. Mirabell opens the black box and saves the situation.

Epilogue – Divides the audience into three classes. High opinion of satire expressed.

Besides these, there is the Dedication which praises Terence for his structure but says he had great examples to follow, like Menander, and supporters like Scipio.

This short synopsis does not by any means give any indication of the impression of complexity the play gives. Literary critics, as has been already said, have not examined the plot very carefully. In this respect, the comments of D.L. Hirst are the most pertinent. First of all, he says that the development of the plot depends largely on events in the past, not in the present:

> The development of the plot depends throughout on the complexity of relationships which have a history stretching back long prior to the play's action.[1]

This is very significant because it gives a historical perspective to the play—historical not in real life but the history of the play. This itself gives it a sense of completeness, like being a world within itself. (i) Mirabell and Millamant have been in love for a long time, (ii) Fainall had married a rich widow for her wealth, (iii) he had been cuckolded by his wife at the time of marriage, (iv) Mrs. Fainall and Mirabell had been intimate at one time but are just good friends now, (v) Mrs. Marwood had a relationship with Fainall for quite some time, and (vi) Mirabell had courted Lady Wishfort to conceal his love for Millamant from her. All these things had happened in the past, and present and future actions grow out of them.

The second observation he has to make about the plot is equally valuable. According to him, all the actions in *The W.W.* proceeds according to precise rules provided by documents and contracts. There are concrete and legally valid reasons for all the turns and twists in the plot:

> The resolution of the plot is brought about according to very precise rules defined by documents and contracts.[2]

These legal overtones are there right from the very beginning. In the Chocolate House after their card play Mirabell talks about the legal hold Lady Wishfort has over Millamant in that she has valid control over half of her fortune. Let alone all the other references to legal contracts, the Bargaining Scene itself has the tones of a legal contract. After she has given her conditions, Millamant says:

> These articles subscribed, if I continue to endure you a little longer, I may by degrees dwindle into a wife.[3]

It is as if she is talking about a legal contract. Mirabell is not behindhand in his superficial dryness. He too puts his conditions with *Inprimises* and *Items* as in a legal contract:

> Item, I article that you continue to like your own face as long as I shall.[4]

Finally, a few more Items later, he makes it fully a legal contract by saying:

> Then we're agreed. Shall I kiss your hand upon the contract? And here comes one to be a witness to the sealing of the deed.[5]

Thus, it is a legal contract sealed with a kiss and with a witness also. Later too, there are numerous references to contracts and legal documents. Finally, there comes the last scene with its black box and papers. The black box has several papers, the most important being the one, signed by Witwoud and Petulant and acknowledged by them. In it Mrs. Fainall, before she got married and was mistress of her own property, made Mirabell her trustee, to whom she gave power over all her property:

> What's here? Damnation! (Reads) "A deed of conveyance of the whole estate real of Arabella Languish, widow, in estate real of Arabella Languish, widow, in trust to Edward Mirabell". Confusion![6]

This is the legal contract that finally defeats Fainall, and at the end, just before the closing Senecan couplets, Mirabell gives it back to Mrs. Fainall:

> Let me before these witnesses restore to you the deed to trust; it may be a means, well-managed, to make you live easily together.[7]

Apart from D.L. Hirst, the other critics have not made any valuable contributions to the discussion. Dobrée for example talks more about the style than about the plot. The only observation he has to make is about the denouement:

> The denouement is forced, a mere trumped up affair, but it does not matter.[8]

Allardyce Nicoll also does not have any praise for the plot:

> We may say that the plot of the play is no plot, only a series of often impossible and confusing incidents designed to afford the author opportunity for regaling us with his stream of conceited metaphors and the bewildering flights of his fancy.[9]

In other words, Nicoll also, while talking about the plot, is diverted to comment upon his style. Indeed, it is difficult to find a critic who can talk about this feature of his play, without being diverted to his style. But his comment on the plot, apart from the reference to style, is nothing if not disparaging, for he says that the events are impossible and confusing and serve only as occasions for his wit. Unfortunately, he does not explain or even refer to, these "impossible and confusing incidents", so the reader is not sure of what he is talking about—are all the incidents impossible and confusing? From that point of view Mirabell's plan with Waitwell and Foible does seem a little far-fetched as, indeed, does the marriage-scheme of Lady Wishfort. They definitely seem rather strange and confusing.

C.T. Thomas devotes pages to the detailed analysis of the action but has nothing very decisive to say about the plot. Yet what he says about it is pithy and succinct:

> The action centres on Lady Wishfort's design to frustrate their love and Mirabell's clever stratagem to outwit the old lady which ultimately is fruitful.[10]

"Their love" of course means the love of Mirabell and Millamant and the sentence makes it clear that there are two actions that are intertwined: (i) Lady Wishfort's plan and (ii) Mirabell's plan. The two go along side by side and that is the reason the play seems confusing. Besides, several side-issues are involved. Sir Wilfull Witwoud's courtship of Millamant, and Fainall's affair with Mrs. Marwood serve to increase the confusion. But it is clear that there are two main actions in the play. It is because the other critics get diverted by the style again and again that they lose sight of the main issue. Congreve refers in the Dedication to Terence and Ben Jonson and this does not help matters as both are master-craftsmen and one expects him to follow in their footsteps. But he does not actually do so. He tangles up the two plots and they are so very much mixed that it is difficult to untwine them. As a result, the play gives the impression of confusion.

References

1. Hirst, D.L., *op. cit.*, p. 32.
2. *Ibid.*, p. 33.
3. IV, p. 86, ll. 220-21.
4. IV, p. 86, ll. 240-41.
5. IV, p. 88, ll. 277-79.
6. V, p. 121, ll. 550-53.
7. V, p. 123, ll. 616-18.
8. Dobrée, *op. cit.*, p. 148.
9. Nicoll, A., *British Drama*, Indian rpt., 1973, Delhi, p. 161.
10. p. 141.

8

Imagery in *The W.W.*

It is usually poetic plays that are rich in imagery and therefore, in their case imagery is an important topic. Plays written in prose are not usually discussed from this point of view. But Congreve's style is so exceptional that one is justified in writing about the images in his plays.

Images are pictures in words. A painter paints a picture with colour and a writer, whether in poetry or in prose, has only to write with words. Defining images Henri Fluchère says:

> Imagery may shortly be defined as a concrete illustration drawn upon by the poet to clarify or embellish the object that he seeks to describe.[1]

The most obvious images are sense-images. There are five kinds of images for our five senses. Thus:

Images pertaining to the eye—visual images.
Images pertaining to the ear—auditory images.
Images pertaining to the nose—olfactory images.
Images pertaining to the tongue—gustatory images.
Images pertaining to the skin—tactile images.

Besides these, there is another kind of sense-image in which more than one sense is involved, known as synaesthesia. There is a special quality about sense-images. Most of the time a sense-image involves another image like a nature image or some other. The very first image in the Prologue of *The W.W.* is one such in the first line:

> Of those few fools, who with ill stars are cursed.[2]

Here "Stars" is a visual image because stars are seen. But it is also a stellar or astronomical image.

Besides sense-images, there are images to be taken from all spheres of life. There are images from nature, domestic life, the trades, etc. Here a few images from the first Act will be mentioned and a few more cases, where the image is so remarkable that it should be commented upon.

Congreve's images are complex ones for they mean much more than they say. Thus, the very first image in the first Act runs thus:

> The coldness of a losing gamester lessens the pleasure of the winner. I'd no more play with a man that slights his ill fortune than I'd make love to a woman who under-values the loss of her reputation.[3]

Here the first image is that of gambling. "Coldness" is not exactly a tactile image because it means mental indifference. In the next sentence, there is an image of a woman of easy virtue. But it is a complex one as it carries moral overtones.

In the next sentence, "a taste extremely delicate" is a gustatory image, but since it means mental taste rather than physical it is again a complex one.

Very often more than one image is involved in a sentence. Thus, Mirabell speaks of Lady Wishfort:

> ...and when she lay in of a dropsy, persuaded her she was reported to be in labour.[4]

Here there is a medical image ("dropsy") as well as a maternity image ("in labour").

These are ordinary images taken for illustrating certain points. Now we shall take up well-known ones. But it should always be remembered that his images are hardly ever ordinary. Fluchère takes account of this when talking of Shakespeare's images:

> No strict rule allows us to say at what point we pass from the plane of pure rhetoric to the plane of pure psychology and even the metaphysical, plane in the use of imagery.[5]

It may seem extravagant to mention Shakespeare while referring to Congreve but let it be kept in mind that Dryden did the same. As quoted earlier, he had said that prodigal nature:

To Shakespeare gave as much, she could not give him more.

So, it is not crossing the limits to mention Shakespeare when talking of Congreve, though his images here will not be studied as extensively as the former's has been.

Now let us take up some well-known images from elsewhere in the play. There is the one in which Mirabell describes the weakness of Lady Wishfort for marriage and for appearing young:

> An old woman's appetite is depraved like that of a girl. 'Tis the green sickness of a second childhood, and like the faint offering of a latter spring, serves but to usher in the fall, and withers in an affected bloom.[6]

"Green sickness" is a medical image, "second childhood" is an image of unnatural senility, "spring" and "fall" are both nature images and "affected bloom" again a nature image with a hint of falsity in it. All in all, it is an image of unnaturalness in human beings and nature and carries a suggestion of falsity about it. All are visual images. The first sentence heightens this sense of falsity, for that which is natural in a young girl is unnatural in a fifty-five years old woman.

A line after this comes Mirabell's description of Millamant, a famous description and a famous image also, one in which rhetoric mixes with imagery, as Fluchère had observed:

> Here she comes, i' faith, full-sail, with her fan spread and her streamers out, and a shoal of fools for tender. Ha, no, I cry her mercy.[7]

This is a very complex image and needs careful reading. First of all, it is, in all, the image of a ship. Had it been a simile it could have been called a Homeric simile. But it is a metaphor and corresponds, point for point, with the object compared. But before taking up these details it should be pointed out that here there is either conscious and deliberate reference to Milton or influence of him, for it echoes Milton's description of Dalila (or

Delilah) in *Samson Agonistes*, ll. 713-19. The relevant lines have been already quoted earlier. Here more details will be given now.

The image corresponds point for point with the thing compared. "Streamers" means flags or pennants that ships fly to point out their identity. Here it corresponds with the lappets of Millamant's head-dress. "Tenders" are small boats that attend on a large one and here it refers to Witwoud who is accompanying Millamant ("a shoal of fools").

Here rhetoric has become one with imagery for actually it is both the visual, nautical image of a ship and a metaphor in which a lady is being compared with a ship. If all the points of comparison are taken one by one, then it can be called an extended metaphor just like a Homeric simile. It is a justly famous description.

The image is continued in the next sentence, which heightens its effect. Mrs. Fainall says:

> I see but one poor empty sculler, and he tows her woman after him.[8]

A sculler is a small boat following a large one and here it refers to Witwoud who is accompanied by ("tows") Mincing, Millamant's maid. In this it makes the image of the ship even stronger. Such an image justifies comparison with imagery in poetry of high order.

Sometime after this, after some sparkling dialogue with more images there is a special one:

> A fellow that lives in a windmill has not a more whimsical dwelling than the heart of a man that is lodged in a woman. There is no point of the compass to which they cannot turn, and by which they are not turned, and by one as another, for motion, not method, is their occupation.[9]

Here the overall image is that of a windmill a visual and a mechanical image, for a windmill is a machine, turned usually by a flowing stream or wind. A man enslaved by a woman is supposed to be living inside a windmill. A windmill is here being imagined as being in a constant state of unrest, being turned this way and that all the time. In addition, it is a random motion, because there is no method in it, it is subject to the turns and twists of the wind. This image of a windmill is complex as it is actually an image dealing with a state of restlessness and it is not a straightforward image merely of a windmill, but that of a man inside it. A state of unrest is the main idea here—an abstract idea, expressed through the concrete image of a machine in random motion.

The play continues in this vein, with sparkling dialogues and brilliant imagery but there are not any more specially notable ones. There is Foible's famous witty remark about her picture to Lady Wishfort but however witty it may be, image-wise it is not remarkable. A detailed study of the play from the point of view of imagery alone will no doubt reveal many treasures, but this is not the place for such a study.

References

1. Fluchère, Henri, *Shakespeare*, London, Longmans, Green & Co., 1953, p. 167.
2. Prologue, l. 1.
3. I, p. 9, ll. 6-10.
4. I, pp. 11-12, ll. 75-76.
5. Fluchère, *op. cit.*, p. 167.
6. II, p. 42, ll. 312-15.
7. II, p. 42, ll. 317-19.
8. II, p. 42, ll. 320-21.
9. II, p. 48, ll. 482-87.

9
Prose Style in the Play

Congreve's prose style is so remarkable that it has often been compared with that of Flaubert for its precision and clarity. Much more is involved in his prose than just wit, though that of course is an integral part of it. There is hardly any critic who has not remarked on it, while Dobrèe, of course, has commented on his prose style much as one does on poetic style. We shall first have a look at Dobrèe's comments and then mention other critics.

Before commenting on Congreve's style himself, Dobrée quoted others who support his own ideas. Thus, he gives Hazlitt's opinion who says that *The W.W.* is:

> ...an essay almost too fine, and the sense of pleasure evaporates in an aspiration after something that seems too exquisite even to have been realized.[1]

Dobrée follows it with his own comment:

> He was the first, apart from the men of Congreve's day, to realize him as a poet, with a poet's longing for beauty.[2]

Then, after quoting Macaulay and Henley (both in praise of his style), he quotes Meredith's famous passage:

> He hits the mean of a fine style and a natural in dialogue. He is at once precise and voluble.... In this he is a classic and is worthy of treading a measure with Molière.[3]

But all this is as nothing to what Dobrée himself has to say, for he looks upon Congreve as a poet. It is true that he takes him very seriously, saying again and again that his aims were very high, moral, satirical, etc., but he lays stress, again and again, on the creation of beauty also:

> In it glows the true Congreve, the Congreve to whom detraction is wearisome, and who aspires after that very fragile thing, beauty itself...we are reminded of a Frenchman, not of Molière...but of Flaubert. The aspiration is the same, the dislike of human folly is the same; there is the identical feeling that the highest achievement is the creation of beauty through the quality and texture of words.... This is his great aim, the creation of beauty by plastic means.[4]

Then he goes on to give examples, quoting from the play. Mirabell and Fainall are talking about fools going on the Grand Tour, and then comments on it:

> "'Tis better to trade with a little loss, than to be quite eaten up with being overstocked". That is a perfect phrase, concise, but without the least suspicion of a rattle—and marvellous in balance.[5]

He does not stop here. In the very next sentence, he goes on to analyse the sentence as if it were poetry and says quite clearly:

The vowel-sounds are carefully selected, so that those in the second part of the sentence echo yet without repeating, those of the first. That is how poetry is written.[6]

He is all the time stressing the poetic beauty of Congreve's style, and in truth he is quite justified. This is how Waitwell, only a servant, speaks to Lady Wishfort and Dobrée comments on it:

> "Dear Madam, no. You are all camphire and frankincense, all chastity and odour". On the stage, no.... Like good poetry, it speaks to the inward ear.[7]

The refinement of language, its poetic beauty according to Dobrée is one of the reasons why *The W.W.* was a failure on the stage:

> If to refine upon existence was Congreve's dominant desire, as it would appear, there was no more for him to do in the world of comedy. He had tried to invest it with the delicacy of drawing-room poetry, and had failed.[8]

Dobrée, thus, treats his style as one would treat poetry. But he is not the only one to be enchanted with it. All critics agree about the beauty of the style of *The W.W.* Thus, Allardyce Nicoll talks of:

> ...regaling us with his stream of conceited metaphors and the bewildering flights of his fancy...his power lay, not in the fashioning of dramatic incidents, but in his mastery of wit and in his command of dancing words. The melodies charm our ears:
>
> Mir.: Do you lock yourself up from me to make my search more curious? Or is the pretty artifice contrived to signify that here the chase must end, and my pursuit be crowned, for you can fly no more?
>
> Mill.: Vanity! I will fly and be followed to the last moment: though I am upon the very verge of matrimony, I expect you should solicit me as if I were wavering at the grate of a monastery.[9]

So Nicoll talks of "dancing words" and of melody charming our ears. Again, these are phrases that are usually applied to poetry, and he quotes the whole of the Bargaining Scene in support.

In the text being used C.T. Thomas, after referring to Dryden, Dobrée and Schelling has this to say of Congreve's inimitable style:

> In Congreve there is hardly a superfluous word or expression. Each word is chosen with meticulous care for its sound and glitter. The sentences are equally perfect, the similitudes cunningly worked out and the repartees are always memorable. Congreve's dialogues are meant to be spoken...the carefully balanced structure, the pointed phrase, the alliteration and antithetical expression attaining their full nuance. The rhythm and cadence of his speeches.... The beauty of his style relies very largely on the quality and the texture of his words. Congreve arranges his vowels and his consonants with the same care that a musician bestows on the arrangement of his notes.[10]

Then, instead of giving quotations from the play, he quotes Dobrée and Hazlitt but it is noticeable that he particularly mentions certain points of style such as:

(1) carefully balanced structure
(2) the pointed phrase
(3) alliteration
(4) antithesis
(5) arrangement of vowels
(6) arrangement of consonants

We can illustrate, though he does not, these points from the play itself.

(1) Carefully balanced structure

> I'd no more play with a man that slights his ill fortune than I'd make love to a woman who undervalues the loss of her reputation.[11]

Here the two parts of the sentence have been marked with double vertical lines. The parts are balanced.

(2) The pointed phrase

> She who does not refuse them everything
> can refuse em nothing.[12]

The two-pointed phrases are separated by a vertical line. It is also an example of balanced structure.

(3) Alliteration

> 'Tis pity, faith; the fellow has fire and life.[13]

Here the letter "f" is repeated as the initial letter in three words in the same sentence.

(4) Antithesis

> Aye, aye, friendship without freedom is as dull as love without enjoyment or wine without toasting.[14]

There are at least three antitheses in this sentence.

(5) Arrangement of vowels

> Though I am upon the very verge of matrimony, I expect you should solicit me as much as it I were hovering at the

> gate of monastery, with one foot over the threshold. I'll be solicited to the very last, nay, and afterwards.[15]

In these two sentences, the vowels have been so arranged as to make the enunciation of the lines easy and natural, smooth and colloquial.

(6) Arrangement of consonants

The above quotation can be taken as a masterly arrangement of consonants also. The repetition of "v" in "very verge" and of "s" in "should solicit" are the most obvious, but apart from that, the use of liquid consonants like "m", "n", "l" and "r" make the lines easy and smooth.

Apart from these features, there is the use of stylistic devices like figures of speech, symbols and images to be considered. Imagery has been already dealt with in the foregoing chapter. There are no symbols important enough to be discussed. Rhetoric is a different matter. An analysis of the figures of speech, even a brief account, will be a long study. So only a few remarkable instances will be quoted here. Alliteration and antithesis have been already commented upon earlier.

In the Bargaining Scene, Millamant says:

> My dear liberty, shall I leave thee? My faithful solitude, my darling contemplation, must I bid you then adieu?[16]

In these sentences, we have three figures of speech in one: rhetorical question, apostrophe and personification. In the first sentence, for example, she is personifying liberty, apostrophising it (i.e. addressing it directly) and asking a question that does not need an answer, but automatically answers itself. The same thing is done in the next sentence and this feature is continued in the next sentence which has not been quoted.

Not all the figures of speech are quite so remarkable as this one but there are many very good figures of speech employed. There is a hyperbole used by Millamant:

> Oh, I hate a lover that can dare to think he draws a moment's air independent on the bounty of his mistress.[17]

This is a very charming hyperbole. Though it starts negatively ("I hate"), it is nevertheless a most charming hyperbole. It is an exaggeration of the Petrarchan mode of idealised love and idealized mistress.

Mirabell also employs some remarkable figures:

> An old woman's appetite is depraved like that of a girl. 'Tis the green sickness of a second childhood; and like the first offering of a latter spring, serves but to usher in the fall and withers in an affected bloom.[18]

This is a most complex figure of speech because it is the combination of several similes and metaphors. The first sentence is a simile. The next sentence can be seen as a continuation of the same simile containing within itself another simile ("like the first offering", etc.). If it is looked upon as a simile then it is a Homeric simile. If, on the other hand, the sentence is taken to be independent of the first sentence then it is a metaphor and, as such, a metaphor that merges later into a simile. It is a most complex figure of speech.

Congreve's style is thus a very rich and poetic and complex one and is well worth a far more extensive study than has been done here.

Versification

Like all Restoration comedies, the play is written in prose but, though very little, there is some versification in it. Besides the Senecan couplets there are the songs and the Prologue and the Epilogue.

There are, in all, six Senecan couplets, one at the end of each Act and two at the end of Act V. The first of them is at the end of the Act I:

> Where modesty's ill manners, 'tis but fit
> That impudence and malice pass for wit

This couplet, spoken by Mirabell, can be taken to sum up Congreve's own attitude to these plays or wit. He makes use of even stichomythia in his couplets. Thus, at the end of Act IV, we have:

> Waitwell: E'er long you shall substantial proof receive
> That I'am an arrant knight—
> Foible: or arrant knave.

There are a few songs in the play as well, four songs, to be exact. The first of them is in Act III, sc. xii. It is a traditional love-song, a love-song in the cavalier manner with three stanzas. The others are all drinking songs, sung by Sir Wilfull Witwoud when drunk. They are written like Elizabethan drinking song. Elizabethan plays all had such songs, even tragedies. In this scene (IV: x), there are two of them and another in the following. It differs from Elizabethan songs in having some topical references such as "tea-cups and coffee" in the third song. They cannot be found in Elizabethan songs.

The Prologue and the Epilogue are in heroic couplets. They are polished and regular with occasional triplets. The audience is condemned in the Epilogue for criticizing the play without understanding it. The Prologue tells us about the play itself and its plot. The important lines have been already quoted earlier. He writes about the different features of the play, about how they have been executed by him. He writes briefly and with great modesty:

> Some plot we think he has and some new thought
> Some humour too, no farce, but that's a fault.

These lines have already been commented upon on other occasions, so this is not done now. Since for every quotation the source is already given in the sentences preceding it, detailed reference is not given.

References

1. Quoted by Dobrée, *op. cit.,* p. 121.
2. *Ibid.*, p. 122.
3. *Ibid.*
4. *Ibid.*, p. 138.
5. *Ibid.*, p. 139.
6. *Ibid.*
7. *Ibid.*, pp. 142-43.
8. *Ibid.*, p. 149.
9. Nicoll, A., *op. cit.*, pp. 161-62.
10. C, p. 140.
11. I, p. 9, ll. 8-10.

12. I, p. 12, ll. 88-89.
13. I, p. 22, ll. 293-94.
14. I, p. 24, ll. 347-48.
15. IV, p. 84, ll. 151-55.
16. IV, p. 84, ll. 176-78.
17. IV, p. 84, ll. 165-67.
18. II, p. 42, ll. 312-15.

10

Critical Reception of the Play

It is a well-known fact that at the time of performance *The W.W.* was a stage failure which discouraged Congreve from writing plays any more, and he retired from the stage at the early age of thirty. He himself was so highly estimated that Dryden compared him with Shakespeare but *The W.W.* was undoubtedly a failure on the stage.

The first systematic study we have of him is in the eighteenth century, by Dr. Johnson, though he considered him as a poet not as a dramatist. Yet what he has to say is extremely important. His views have been already quoted in different contexts before this:

> ...he is an original writer, who borrowed neither the models of his plot, nor the manner of his dialogue...his characters are commonly fictitious and artificial, with very little of nature and not much of life.... His scenes exhibit not much of humour, imagery or passion: his personages are a kind of intellectual gladiators; every sentence is to ward or strike...his wit is a meteor playing to and fro with alternate coruscations. His comedies have, therefore, in some degree, the operation of tragedies; they surprise rather than divert, and raise admiration oftener than merriment.[1]

These remarks have already been discussed in details elsewhere. Let it be remarked here that he gives brief but important remarks on every aspect of his plays: plot, character, style, function, genre, etc. Before him we do not have such comprehensive consideration at all, and the remarks have been, each of them, much commented upon.

The fact that the play was a failure is difficult to understand today as in his own day he was held in high esteem, if not overestimated. Dryden had roundly declared:

> However, that but once was prodigal before,
> To Shakespeare gave as much; she could not give him more.[2]

This position has, more or less, been held by him. The early nineteenth-century critics did not overestimate him but were loud in praise of him. Coleridge was perhaps the only detractor. Hazlitt wrote:

> *The Way of the World* has an essence almost too fine, and the sense of pleasure evaporates in an aspiration after something that seems too exquisite ever to have been realized.[3]

Dobrée, quoting this, points out quite rightly that Hazlitt was the first critic to realize the poetic possibilities of his style and point out its refinements. A far more serious view of Congreve was taken by Coleridge. He did not talk so much about the style as about the content. According to him, Congreve treated comedy far too seriously, more seriously than it should be taken:

> Wickedness is no subject for comedy. This was Congreve's greatest error and peculiar to him. The dramatic personages of Dryden, Wycherley and others are often viciously indecent but not, like Congreve's wicked.[4]

This, indeed, is a famous critical concept of Coleridge's and one of his finest. It shows real penetration of the subject-matter and nature of comedy as well as that of Congreve. It is perfectly true as far as *The W.W.*, with which we are particularly concerned, the villains are concerned. Mrs. Marwood who can surely be called the villainess, retains her villainy to the last, stepping into the plot again and again to throw obstacles in Mirabell's way and making a fool of Lady Wishfort at every step to the top of her bent. This is even truer of Fainall who remains a villain till the very end. He is truly wicked as Coleridge would say. Even when almost all hope is gone, he holds a sword over Lady Wishfort's head. Only when the black box is opened and the document appointing Mirabell as the trustee of his wife's property is discovered, he is finally defeated and tries to attack his wife.

The most important critical contribution to the views on Restoration comedy in the nineteenth century is undoubtedly that of Lamb. The last of his *Essays of Elia* were published in 1833. One of them was entitled "On the Artificial Comedy of the Last Century" and it was in this that he expounded his theory that the world they depict is an unreal one. It is an entirely imaginary, an "artificial" one:

> It is altogether a speculative scene of things which has no reference whatever to the world that is.[5]

In a way, he approves of it, as it is so different from the intensely moral tone of contemporary drama. He is of the opinion that the artificial, unrealistic, a-moral world of the comedy of manners affords a relief from the heavy morality of contemporary drama:

> I am glad for a reason to take an air beyond the diocese of a strict conscience.[6]

He even defends these plays from the criticism of Coleridge who had specially singled out Congreve:

> We are not to judge them by our usages
> ...there is neither right nor wrong, gratitude
> or its opposite, claim or duty, paternity or sonship.[7]

Not everyone had so much critical insight as Coleridge had but the other critics of the nineteenth century also did not have much to say in defence of Congreve. Thus, Leigh Hunt remarks:

> We see nothing but a set of heartless fine ladies and gentlemen coming in and going out, saying witty things at each other and buzzing in some maze of intrigue.[8]

This is not systematic criticism; it is just like a passing remark. All the same it is noticeable that Leigh Hunt does talk about (a) lack of sincerity, (b) wit and (c) intrigue.

Macaulay remarks on his epigrammatic style:

> In this sort of jewelry he attained to a mastery unprecedented and inimitable.[9]

As a matter of fact, besides Coleridge, the other critics, when critically remarking on him, talk about his style. Thus Henley says:

> He is saved from oblivion by the sheer strength of style.[10]

Meredith's passage on Congreve is well known. It deals with his style more in detail:

> He hits the mean of a fine style and a natural in dialogue. He is at once precise and voluble.... In this he is a classic, and is worthy of treading a measure with Molière.[11]

This has already been quoted and commented upon earlier. It is noticeable that he talks about his dialogue and points out that it has several characteristics: (a) naturalness, (b) precision, and (c) volubility. The first of these qualities is a must for drama but the next two might seem to be mutually exclusive at first glance. How can precision and volubility go together? But for Congreve it is quite true.

Against this may be placed another remark, that of Whibley, who says almost the opposite of what Meredith does ("volubility") and praises his highly economical style:

> In point and concision, his style is still unmatched in the literature of England. There is never a word too much, or an epithet that is superfluous.[12]

This, again, is perfectly true. Indeed, his style is so complex that whatever may be said in praise of it is too little. This has been recognised by critics of all ages, his own as well as those of a much later one.

In the twentieth century, the first critic to be considered is, of course, Dobrée. He makes a systematic survey of all the different aspects of his play, though he too gives pride of place to his style. First of all, he divides comedy into three classes: (a) Critical comedy, (b) "Free" comedy, and (c) Great comedy, and places Congreve's plays in the first category. This point has already been discussed earlier in some detail under the topic of "Genre", so it is not necessary to go into details here, suffice it to say that this kind of comedy criticises society and lays stress on morality:

> It expresses the general feeling of the community, for which another name is morality; it is, to quote Meredith again, "guardian" of our civil fortune...it supports the happy mean.... Its lesson is to be righteous, but not to be righteous overmuch.... Its object is to damp enthusiasm, to prick illusions.[13]

After explaining the nature of critical comedy, Dobrée turns to Congreve and observes of his plays:

> The thread of sadness and disillusion runs through these plays and live passions break through the veil of cynicism wherewith the critical comedy clothes itself.[14]

Thus, explaining the spirit of the three early plays he turns to *The W.W.* itself:

> *The Way of the World* is his masterpiece of literary art, as well as his final vindication of mankind. In it glows the true Congreve, the Congreve to whom detraction is wearisome, and who aspires after that very fragile thing, beauty itself.[15]

After this, he analyses *The W.W.*, speaking of its style, wit, plot, character and theme. Of some aspects he speaks in detail, and only cursorily on some. These comments have all been quoted and commented upon in the relevant places in earlier chapters. But the final conclusion he reaches is a negative one:

> ...in spite of his excelling qualities, one must confess failure if we judge by the greatest standards. His criticism never won through to a broader vision; his disillusion conquered him.[16]

Besides Dobrée, the others also, even if they do not study the play in detail, agree about its perfection. Thus, Allardyce Nicoll is of the opinion:

> Only perhaps in *The Way of the World* is Congreve able to reach complete perfection. Here there is no false note. Millamant sails gloriously through its scenes.... We may say that the plot of the play is no plot, only a series of often impossible and confusing incidents designed to afford the author opportunity for regaling us with his stream of

> conceited metaphors and the bewildering flights of his fancy...his power lay, not in the fashioning of dramatic incidents but in his mastery of wit and in his command of dancing words.[17]

So here again we find stress being laid on "dancing words" and "mastery of wit" rather than on plot and character. In fact, Nicoll denies that there is any well-constructed plot at all. It has been already pointed out, in connection with this remark, in the chapter on Plot (Chap. 7) that it is not true that there is no plot. In fact, there are two plots, but they are so mixed up, or intertwined, that the result seems to be confusing.

As for "conceited metaphors" they have already been extensively commented upon in Chap. 9.

Schelling, agreeing with the view that it is "artificial comedy" because it is:

> ...less and less transcription of life.... Congreve's first comedy was written before he knew anything of actual fashionable life and his last respects, as cynically, if more elaborately, precisely the same sort of personages, the same intrigues and situations.[18]

He then quotes with approval William Archer's views:

> ...a picture of society observed from a standard of complete moral indifference.[19]

He calls the world of the play "the foul and glittering utopia". He does not have anything positive to say even about *The W.W.* His opinion of it is given in the quotation given immediately before the last ("his last repeats", etc.).

Among later critics of the twentieth century, D.L. Hirst's opinion is of value because he considers the play in a truly critical spirit. He has valuable remarks to make on the plot, the theme as well as on wit.

Thus, he remarks:

> From the start it is clear that every person in this play is involved in a ruthless battle of wits in which the stakes are very high.[20]

His remark on the plot is equally valuable as he sees it in a completely different manner:

> The development of the plot depends throughout on the complexity of relationships which have a history stretching back long prior to the play's action.[21]

Thus, he places the plot against a perspective in the circumstances of the play itself. About the theme, he sees again an interaction of financial and sexual motives:

> From the start sexual and monetary motives are seen to be closely related and moreover, to determine entirely the development of the action.[22]

Another pertinent remark of his concerns the plot, that it has a legal aspect:

> The resolution of the plot is brought about according to very precise rules defined by documents and contracts.[23]

He justifies all these claims by giving definite instances from the play and comes to the conclusion:

> It remains our most complete and subtle comedy of manners and a reminder that essentially the genre begins where Shakespeare and his contemporaries end: with marriage.[24]

All these comments have been extensively discussed in the relevant chapters (Chaps. 3, 5 and 7 for Genre, Theme and Plot respectively).

Thus, whether in his own time or later, Congreve's plays, especially *The W.W.*, have received universal critical acclaim. Since all of these views have been discussed in the foregoing chapters they have not been discussed here, only passing mention has been made.

References

1. Dr. Johnson, *op. cit.*, p. 30.
2. Quoted by Dobrée, *op. cit.*, p. 121.
3. *Ibid.*
4. *Ibid.*, p. 122.
5. Quoted in D.L. Hirst, *op. cit.*, p. 48.

6. *Essays of Elia*, pp. 165-72, Quoted in Hirst, *ibid.*
7. *Ibid.*
8. Quoted by Dobrée, *op. cit.*, p. 122.
9. *Ibid.*
10. *Ibid.*
11. *Ibid.*
12. *Ibid.*
13. *Ibid.*, p. 11.
14. *Ibid.*, p. 138.
15. *Ibid.*
16. *Ibid.*, p. 150.
17. Nicoll, A., *op. cit.*, pp. 161-62.
18. Schelling, F., *op. cit.*, p. 268.
19. *Ibid.*
20. Hirst, D.L., *op. cit.*, p. 31.
21. *Ibid.*, p. 32.
22. *Ibid.*, p. 33.
23. *Ibid.*
24. *Ibid.*, p. 35.

Some Important Passages for Explanation with Reference to the Context from the Play

The text is the one that has been used all along, i.e. the one edited by C.T. Thomas (reference being given as Congreve).

1. The Coldness of .... her reputation. (I, p, 9. ll. 6-10)
2. The discovery .... of nature. (I, p. 11, ll. 64-6)
3. I confess .... 'em nothing. (I, p. 12, ll. 85-89)
4. She has beauty .... tell her so. (I, p. 14, ll. 149-51)
5. And for .... more agreeable. (I, p. 15, ll. 154-59)
6. They are .... as well. (I, p. 15, ll. 169-71)
7. No matter .... of all ages. (I, p. 16, ll. 194-96)
8. I wonder .... of fools. (I, p. 16, ll. 197-99)
9. But when .... want wit. (I, p. 17, ll. 212-15)
10. I beg pardon .... the world. (I, p. 18, ll. 250-52)
11. A wit .... of beauty. (I, p. 21, ll. 314-16)
12. Friendship without freedom .... without toasting. (I, p. 22, ll. 347-48)
13. Oh, raillery .... or me. (I, p. 26, ll. 434-37)
14. Whether this uncle .... faith. (I, p. 27, ll. 473-77)
15. Where modesty's .... for wit. (I, p. 29, ll. 428-29)
16. Men are .... fly from us. (II, p. 30, ll. 3-9)
17. But say .... my possession. (II, p. 30, ll. 12-18)
18. He has .... us both. (II, p. 34, ll. 98-103)
19. Nothing remains .... to conquer. (II, p. 34, ll. 110-12)

20. To let you know .... your eyes. (II, p. 35, ll. 131-36)
21. Shame and .... your bosom. (II, pp. 36-37, ll. 167-74)
22. By all .... of wealth. (II, p. 37, ll. 191-94)
23. And wherefore .... and you. (II. p. 38, ll. 203-05)
24. I'll hate .... he pacified. (II, p. 39, ll. 240-43)
25. Why do we .... reputation. (II, p. 40, ll. 259-60)
26. A better man .... remedy. (II, p. 40, ll. 270-73)
27. If your mother .... beforehand. (II, p. 41, ll. 287-90)
28. Female Frailty .... is decayed. (II, p. 42, ll. 309-11)
29. An old woman's .... affected bloom. (II, p. 42, ll. 312-15)
30. Here she comes .... tenders. (II, p. 42, ll. 317-18)
31. Long! Lord .... new fashion. (II, p. 42, ll. 338-40)
32. For your beauty .... your face. (II, p. 45. ll. 385-90)
33. Oh aye, letters .... one's hair. (II, pp. 43-44, ll. 351-54)
34. Beauty .... makes more. (II, p. 45, ll. 394-98)
35. One owes .... a being. (II, p. 45, ll. 402-04)
36. How can you .... of folly. (II, p. 46, ll. 426-30)
37. I say .... and sincerity. (II, p. 47, ll. 454-56)
38. Sententious .... tapestry hanging. (II, p. 47, ll. 457-59)
39. A fellow .... of instinct. (II, p. 48, ll. 482-90)
40. Married .... man again. (II, p. 51, ll. 542-49)
41. Oh, he .... opportunity (III, p. 54, ll. 55-58)
42. I warrant .... for you, madam (III, p. 57, ll. 147-50)
43. I shall die .... is alluring. (III, p. 57, ll. 154-60)
44. For a fool's .... of sense. (III, p. 62, ll. 301-04)
45. O man, man .... rest of him (III, p. 60, ll. 230-33)
46. I'll take my .... discarded toast. (III, p. 63, ll. 315-16)

47. Raillery .... and bass. (III, p. 65, ll. 380-84)
48. And I .... of the world. (III, p. 74, ll. 605-08)
49. Let husbands .... disown the order. (III, p. 77, ll. 690-97)
50. Verity .... afterwards. (IV, pp. 83-84, ii. 150-55)
51. Oh I hate .... pleasure. (IV, p. 84, ll. 165-72)
52. My dear liberty .... adieu. (IV, p. 84, ll. 176-78)
53. And lastly .... a wife. (IV, p. 86, ll. 218-21)
54. Well, you .... a word. (IV, p. 88, ll. 289-92)
55. Well, if .... violently. (IV, p. 89, ll. 310-11)
56. You are .... and odour. (IV, p. 97, ll. 526-27)
57. No damage .... actress. (V, p. 103, ll. 35-48)
58. Not understand .... little enough. (V, p. 107, ll. 148-52)
59. I am content .... flower of knighthood. (V, p. 113, ll. 329-33)
60. If a .... you more. (V, p. 114, ll. 370-79)
61. At least .... future comfort. (V, p. 115, ll. 390-96)
62. Oh, he has .... my breast. (V, pp. 116-17, ll. 436-39)
63. You shall .... covenant. (V, pp. 116-17, ll. 436-39)
64. This My Lady .... can again. (V, p. 117, ll. 444-47)
65. If it must .... the more. (V, p. 118, ll. 476-79)
66. A deed .... Confusion I (V, p. 121, ll. 551-53)
67. Even so .... your lady. (V, p. 121, ll. 554-56)
68. Why does .... over again? (V, p. 123, ll. 592-93)
69. Aye, and over .... my fear. (V, p. 123, ll. 594-97)
70. From hence .... in kind. (V, p. 124, ll. 619-23)

Some Important Questions

1. Is the term "Comedy of Manners" applicable to *The Way of the World*? Give reasons for your answer.
2. What social satire do you find in the play?
3. Comment on the realism of the character portrayal of Mirabell.
4. "Millamant he must have really loved". Do you agree? Justify your answer.
5. Do you think that Fainall is more sinned against than sinning?
6. Coleridge remarked that wickedness is not fit for comedy. How does this apply to *The W.W.*?
7. Comment on the plot-structure of *The W.W.*
8. Write a note on Congreve's wit as found in *The W.W.*
9. Write a note on the imagery employed in *The W.W.*
10. Comment on the term "Artificial Comedy" as applied to *The W.W.* Give reasons for your answer.

A Select Bibliography

The text used in this work is ed. by C.T. Thomas, Cal., 1978.

1. Brown, J.R. and Harris B. (eds.) *Restoration Theatre*, London, 1965.
2. Dobrée, B., *Restoration Comedy*, Oxford, 1924.
3. Hirst, D.L., *Comedy of Manners*, London, 1979
4. Holland, N., *The First Modern Comedy*, Cambr., 1959.
5. Loftis, J., *Comedy and Society from Congreve to Fielding*, Stanford, 1959.
6. —— ed., Restoration Drama, *Modern Essays in Criticism*, New York, 1966.
7. Muir, K., *The Comedy of Manners*, London, 1970.
8. Nicoll, A., *British Drama*, Delhi, 2013.
9. Ogg, D., *England in the Reign of Charles II*, Oxford, 1956.
10. Wilcox, J., *The Relation of Molière to Restoration Comedy*, New York, 1938.

The Atlantic Critical Studies

D.H. Lawrence's ***Sons and Lovers*** by *Atlantic Research Division*, pp. 168, ₹ 495.00

E.M. Forster's ***A Passage to India*** by *Rama Kundu*, pp. 296, 2007, ₹ 550.00

Emily Brontë's ***Wuthering Heights*** by *Jibesh Bhattacharyya*, pp. 192, ₹ 350.00

Ernest Hemingway's ***A Farewell to Arms*** by *P.G. Rama Rao*, pp. 168, ₹ 350.00

Ernest Hemingway's ***The Old Man and the Sea*** by *P.G. Rama Rao*, pp. 160, ₹ 395.00

Jane Austen's ***Pride and Prejudice*** by *Jibesh Bhattacharyya*, pp. 192, ₹ 350.00

Joseph Conrad's ***Heart of Darkness*** by *Mohit Kumar Ray*, pp. 208, ₹ 495.00

Ruth Prawer Jhabvala's ***Heat and Dust*** by *I.H. Shihan*, pp. 160, ₹ 350.00

Salman Rushdie's ***Midnight's Children*** by *Pradip Kumar Dey*, pp. 168, ₹ 395.00

William Golding's ***Lord of the Flies*** by *Santwana Haldar*, pp. 184, ₹ 495.00

William Shakespeare's ***Antony and Cleopatra*** by *Ratri Ray*, pp. 208, ₹ 495.00

William Shakespeare's ***Othello*** by *Jibesh Bhattacharyya*, pp. 232, ₹ 450.00

William Shakespeare's ***The Merchant of Venice*** by *Ratri Ray*, pp. 184, ₹ 375.00

William Shakespeare's ***A Midsummer Night's Dream*** by *Ratri Ray*, pp. 192, ₹ 395.00

William Shakespeare's ***As You Like It*** *by Ratri Ray*, pp. 200, ₹ 450.00

William Shakespeare's ***Hamlet*** by *Ratri Ray*, pp. 216, ₹ 495.00

William Shakespeare's ***Julius Caesar*** by *Ratri Ray*, pp. 200, ₹ 495.00

William Shakespeare's ***King Lear*** by *Ratri Ray*, pp. 184, ₹ 395.00

William Shakespeare's ***Othello*** by *Ratri Ray*, pp. 208, ₹ 395.00

William Shakespeare's ***The Tempest*** by *Ratri Ray*, pp. 192, ₹ 395.00

William Shakespeare's ***Twelfth Night*** by *Ratri Ray*, pp. 224, ₹ 395.00

William Shakespeare's ***Macbeth*** by *Ratri Ray*, pp. 162, ₹ 495.00

Christopher Marlowe's ***Dr. Faustus*** by *Ratri Ray*, pp. 134, ₹ 495.00